David Eldridge Trilogy
Beginning; Middle; End

methuen | drama
LONDON • NEW YORK • OXFORD • NEW DELHI • SYDNEY

METHUEN DRAMA

Bloomsbury Publishing Plc, 50 Bedford Square, London, WC1B 3DP, UK
Bloomsbury Publishing Inc, 1359 Broadway, New York, NY 10018, USA
Bloomsbury Publishing Ireland, 29 Earlsfort Terrace, Dublin 2, D02 AY28, Ireland

BLOOMSBURY, METHUEN DRAMA and the Methuen
Drama logo are trademarks of Bloomsbury Publishing Plc.

First published as a trilogy in Great Britain 2025
Reprinted 2026

Beginning originally published 2017
Middle originally published 2022
End originally published 2025

Copyright © David Eldridge
Introduction Copyright © Dan Rebellato, 2025

David Eldridge has asserted his right under the Copyright, Designs
and Patents Act, 1988, to be identified as author of this work.

Cover design by Megan Wilson

Photograph © Simon Kessler via Unsplash

All rights reserved. No part of this publication may be: i) reproduced or transmitted in any form, electronic or mechanical, including photocopying, recording or by means of any information storage or retrieval system without prior permission in writing from the publishers; or ii) used or reproduced in any way for the training, development or operation of artificial intelligence (AI) technologies, including generative AI technologies. The rights holders expressly reserve this publication from the text and data mining exception as per Article 4(3) of the Digital Single Market Directive (EU) 2019/790.

Bloomsbury Publishing Plc does not have any control over, or responsibility for, any third-party websites referred to or in this book. All internet addresses given in this book were correct at the time of going to press. The author and publisher regret any inconvenience caused if addresses have changed or sites have ceased to exist, but can accept no responsibility for any such changes.

No rights in incidental music or songs contained in the work are hereby granted and performance rights for any performance/presentation whatsoever must be obtained from the respective copyright owners.

All rights whatsoever in this play are strictly reserved and application for performance etc. should be made before rehearsals by professionals and by amateurs to Independent Talent, 40 Whitfield Street, London, W1T 2RH, UK. No performance may be given unless a licence has been obtained. No rights in incidental music or songs contained in the Work are hereby granted and performance rights for any performance/presentation whatsoever must be obtained from the respective copyright owners.

A catalogue record for this book is available from the British Library.

A catalog record for this book is available from the Library of Congress.

ISBN: PB: 978-1-3506-0947-1
ePDF: 978-1-3506-0948-8
eBook: 978-1-3506-0949-5

Series: Modern Plays

Typeset by Mark Heslington Ltd, Scarborough, North Yorkshire
Printed and bound in Great Britain

For product safety related questions contact
productsafety@bloomsbury.com.

To find out more about our authors and books visit
www.bloomsbury.com and sign up for our newsletters.

Holding Your Nerve

Despite being the most honest and truthful British plays of the twenty-first century, David Eldridge's trilogy, *Beginning*, *Middle* and *End*, are extremely deceptive. First, they look simple. Each seems to have a beginning, a middle and an end – in that order. They are naturalistic in style. They appear not to be formally playful, modishly fragmented, metatheatrical. They look straightforward; but they're not. And each one is a two-hander – just two characters, chatting away in one room. They're domestic in subject matter. Perhaps they look easy or even unambitious, but they're not.

These plays are miracles; they are enormous plays, breathtakingly ambitious, dauntingly profound. They might be my favourite plays of the last decade or two. If you've never written a play, it may not be obvious how hard it is to write plays like this. Simplicity – or apparent simplicity – is one of the hardest things a playwright can do. No play is easy to write, but brutality and cynicism probably ask less of the writer than honesty and sincerity. Each of these plays unfolds in real time in a single location over ninety minutes or so. There is nowhere to hide in a play like that. You need to keep your characters in the room and you need to make it almost unbearable for them to stay in the room, and if you cheat, the audience will spot it a mile off. To make this sort of play honest and truthful, you have to be there with your characters – *as* your characters – and you have to see where they go and what they do. You have to commit, trust your instincts and hold your nerve. In *Middle*, Gary says at one point that 'complete honesty' is 'overrated' and, dramatically, sometimes it is; to have someone say exactly what they mean can feel flat and undynamic. But these plays breathe and they take care to find space where honesty can be shattering and daring.

The characters in this trilogy are both artlessly articulate and articulately artless. Certain moments in these plays are nothing much on the page, but in performance are heart-stopping, a sure sign of great theatre writing. The first time I saw *Beginning*, when Danny said, 'It's broken my heart my whole life', I stopped breathing for a while. This awkward man, on his way to middle age, a feeling of failure spreading through him, and he finds it in himself to admit that. Gary, in *Middle*, admitting, 'I think I'm a bit low. I think I've been like for a long time', is the same. In *End*, Julie makes the small, sad confession, 'I've had this notion. It's got me by'. In each case, these lines don't look like much, but when, dear reader, you get to those moments, if you're in the moments as much as I was, they'll tear you apart. And they're artless, in a way. I don't mean they're poorly written; they're not – they're extraordinary. But none of these characters are accustomed to public speaking; they don't have rhetorical skills. The understatement of Gary's 'a bit low'; the sad inadequacy of Julie choosing 'notion' to describe how she imagined her partner's death; Danny's clumsy repetition of 'my'. A lesser writer would 'correct' these lines, make them fuller, more ringing. As a writer, there's probably a voice in you worrying that an audience will think it's *your* artlessness; that voice might urge you either to tidy the line up or make it *more* inarticulate so that the audience sees the gap between you and the character. But David Eldridge always holds his nerve.

He understands the vital theatrical virtue of the plain sentence, especially when that sentence is a kind of truth bomb. 'I went there,' says Danny, 'In my head', and he's saying he contemplated suicide. Alfie tells Julie, 'I kind of went down a rabbit hole. I mean obviously. My heart was exploding', because he's facing his own death. Gary is lost in the world, but he says, brokenly, 'I need a hug. I need comfort'. It's the apparently artlessness of them that is so articulate; these people are out at their limits and they have no use for cleverness.

That's not to say these plays aren't clever. They are fiercely clever and understand the complexity of how we feel, with splinter-sharp insights into the characters' – and our –

emotional lives. 'You think you're the only one that's lonely?' asks *Beginning*'s Danny, somehow both asserting and erasing that loneliness. Maggie in *Middle* recalls her young daughter seeing her, envious and pathetic and crying and starting to cry, too; 'And I thought,' says Maggie with devastating insight, 'my heartache isn't even my own anymore'. And Julie in *End* responds to a memory of infidelity with a line that would almost be Wildean in its paradox, were it not entirely, compellingly true: 'You were the love of my life. You are the love of my life. How could I ever forgive you?' The trilogy begins with Danny lamenting his lack of a radar to other people's emotions, but these plays are all radar.

I think these plays are hard to talk about, hard to write about. Formal experimentation gives you something to discuss, to explain, to debate. It's easier for critics and scholars to feel they have something to do with plays that are jagged, cryptic, contradictory, fragmented. There's also a critical tradition of keeping a certain aesthetic distance, not to get too involved; to observe and analyse and report. But these plays don't work like that; they demand commitment, full-body commitment from their readers and audiences. You need to hold your nerve, trust them, and go with them. I re-read all of these plays when starting to write this piece. Reader, I cried at the end of each one.

These plays love actors and ask commitment from them, too. There are countless beautiful, generous stage directions that give the actor everything and nothing to do. These are from *Middle*: '*Maggie laughs, wants to cry, doesn't. Silence*'; '*Gary gets upset, holds it in. Silence.*' These directions tell the actor what they must show *and* not show *at the same time* and that might seem perverse, impossible, but it gives the actor enormous freedom. I love the direction for Danny and Laura as they tidy up in *Beginning*: '*They're both dying in the silence*'. Again, they have everything they need but it's all silence and absence. *End* tells Julie and Alfie at one extremely tense moment that '*They consider each other*'. It's almost infinitely demanding and endlessly generous. These plays trust actors.

There's a particular stage direction that is repeated, sometimes with small variations, across the trilogy: '*They look at each other for a long time, for as long as you think you can get away with*'. It's a beautiful thing to say; the switch of subjects, from 'they' to 'you', is thrilling in its sudden direct appeal to the actors. It asks them to let the moment take its time, to trust each other, to be truthful.

I'm interested in what that does to the structure and rhythm of the play. Playwrights always need to learn the importance of good structure, but sometimes that can turn into a rather artificial story style – what David once referred to as 'the clonky old form of what's-round-the-corner plotting' – where we anxiously move from twist to revelation to reversal in an unseemly attempt to keep the audience's interest by constantly throwing new things at them. What I like about the directions is that they disrupt that frantic forward movement and they require actors and audience to stay in the moment, in the 'now'. They make everything feel open and unpredictable.

This flexible openness with time threads through the entire texture of the trilogy. Each play has a moment that requires the actors to take their time. There's tidying up in *Beginning* (in fact, in all three plays), destruction in *Middle*, reading messages in *End*. In each case, David's challengingly reassuring direction is, 'It takes as long as it takes'. There's a variant on the 'as long as you can get away with' in *Middle*: '*They stand there holding each other, just holding each other, for as long as you think you can get away with*'. There's a complexity to this, too: for me, the repetition paradoxically erases doubleness, the adverbial 'just' insisting that what they are doing is what they are doing: there's no irony, no theatrical edge, no contrapuntal subtext. They are just holding each other and nothing else. (The moment is prefigured in *Beginning* as Laura dares to express the future she wants – 'Holding hands. Holding hands and never letting go' – and it resurfaces in *End*: '*They hold each other for a long time, just hold each other*'.) Again, we are asked to stay in the moment, not leverage the present against the past or future, just stay in the here and now.

These plays may not seem on the surface experimental, but they do astonishing things with time and that structural openness underpins the emotional experience of the characters. Pretty much all of them begin the play with blank futures; Laura and Danny approaching middle age with uncertainty and unfulfillment; Maggie and Gary's marriage in a rut; Julie and Alfie staring death in the face. But, within the first couple of minutes, each play releases a simple declaration that knocks the scene off its axis: 'I wanted you, Danny'; 'I'm not sure I love you anymore'; 'I've decided I don't want any more treatment'. These moments mess with the audience's sense of time: they both slam the brakes on the situation while they also, somehow, hit the accelerator. The plays then show these characters learning tentatively, painfully, to accept the present, to fully commit to it. 'I care about now,' says Danny in *Beginning*, 'The now. It's all I care about, Laura'. In *End*, we watch as Julie and Alfie *'both use all their willpower and courage to stay present in the room'*. And in committing to the present, which actually means committing to being present to each other, they start to reconcile with the past, put it aside, with forgiveness, gentleness and understanding. And in doing so, they open up their futures. I remember watching *Beginning* as Laura started to express an impossibly fragile but longed-for future with Danny and I felt the future splitting wide open. There are similar moments of emotional daring in all three plays. Indeed, in a sense, all three plays begin with an end (end of a party, of a marriage, of a life) and they end with a beginning (a new relationship, a new hope, a new life). It's why these apparently domestic plays feel emotionally vast, their journeys epic in scale.

They're also not wholly domestic in another sense. They only touch on politics at the edges but they engage profoundly with the peculiarities of Britain's political polarisation since the mid-2010s. The three plays take place in late autumn

2015, February 2016 and June 2016, dates that slowly approach the vote of the UK's membership of the European Union in late June 2016, which, whatever your view of Brexit, undeniably exposed and heightened deep – and, it has sometimes seemed, unbridgeable – divisions in our society. David is very fond of quoting playwright John Osborne's declaration, 'I want to make people feel, to give them lessons in feeling'. When Osborne wrote that in the 1950s, he was responding to a conservative class habit of amused understatement and restraint. Our age is different, perhaps afraid of emotion in a different way, preferring to forestall empathy by demanding it, each of us asserting our own truths from our respective barricade. These plays ask us to make time to take one another seriously, in all our complexity, our strengths and flaws.

It would be easy to write a version of these plays that took refuge in laughter. Don't get me wrong, these are often very funny plays, but when these characters say things that are embarrassingly ridiculous (Gary: 'I think with the sex thing. There's bits and bobs we can do'; Danny: 'I'm a bit poorly maintained in the area of the groin') we cannot just laugh at them, because we also understand the awkwardness and desperation that has produced these maladroit utterances. These characters, foolish and inadequate to the situation as they are at times, have a profound dignity in the writing; they have weight and presence, they stand on their floor. They are never laughable, never contemptible. In part this is about class; David writes about working-class men and women better than any writer of his generation: honestly, respectfully, unsentimentally. But he also writes beautifully about men, and about women, and about men and women. These plays reach out across our cultural divides.

They also reach out to each other. Just as these divided couples miraculously find connection, these plays are haunted by each other. Motifs and moments, ideas and images ripple across the whole trilogy: kiwi fruit, Crouch End, broken china, West Ham, loneliness, Bros, cooking for someone, dancing for someone. There are two songs in *End* that we first heard in *Beginning* or *Middle*. The plays are nourished by each other and together they paint a larger canvas than may at first be apparent, a theatrical landscape that appears to make our hopeless times seem hopeful. The three plays take us through the night, beginning in the early hours, sometime after 4pm and 6.50am, respectively. These plays take us through the night. In a sense, these plays may help us make it through the night.

These plays are astonishing. I'd say that if you want to learn how to write a play, watch and read *Beginning*, *Middle* and *End* over and over and over again. But, more than that, I'd say that if you want to re-learn how to feel, watch and read *Beginning*, *Middle* and *End* over and over and over again, as long as you think you can get away with.

Dan Rebellato

These plays take place in real rooms and in real time – but stage directions are indicative not prescriptive.

Beginning

For Caroline Winder

Beginning was first produced in the Dorfman Theatre at the National Theatre, London, on 12 October 2017. The production transferred to the Ambassadors Theatre in London's West End on 15 January 2018.

Laura	**Justine Mitchell**
Danny	**Sam Troughton**
Director	Polly Findlay
Designer	Fly Davis
Lighting Designer	Jack Knowles
Sound Designer	Paul Arditti
Movement	Naomi Said
Associate Director	Joe Lichtenstein

Late autumn, 2015.

The large living room of a flat in Crouch End, London. It encompasses a lounge area and kitchen.

It's a bit of a mess. There's been some sort of party. It's late, the early hours.

Standing is **Laura**, *38. This is her place. She's drinking wine.*

Looking at her, drinking a bottle of Peroni, is **Danny**, *42.*

They look at each other for a long time, for as long as you think you can get away with.

They both jump as a door bangs downstairs.

He begins to wander a bit in the room, drinking. He evidently came to the party after work as he's in a shirt and trousers and smart shoes. Though his jacket and tie were dispensed some time ago.

He has a big ketchup stain on his shirt and is a bit nervous.

Silence.

Laura *sits down.* **Danny** *doesn't know what to do so he lights up a cigarette.*

Laura You didn't fancy it then?

Silence.

Danny Fancy what?

Laura Getting in the taxi?

Danny No.

Silence.

Laura Why's that then?

Danny Don't know.

Laura Don't know?

Danny Keith told me to stay and finish my drink.

Laura Keith told you?

Danny Well he said 'stay and finish your drink'.

Laura Right.

Danny That all right?

Laura Yes.

Laura *smiles and puts down her wine.*

Danny Nice place.

Laura Thanks.

Danny To be honest I said I'd get it.

Laura Get what?

Danny The taxi.

Laura What?

Silence.

Danny Well, you know . . .

Laura What?

Danny I thought he was stopping the night.

Laura Right.

Laura *laughs.*

Danny You see the trouble with me . . .

Laura What?

Danny I've got no radar.

Laura No radar?

Danny No.

Silence.

Well it's not that I've not got one at all.

Laura   Right?

Danny   It just doesn't pick up a lot.

Silence.

Laura   Danny, what the fuck?

Silence.

Danny   You know, 'your radar'.

Laura   I don't know, Danny.

Danny   Your 'man radar' . . . And my . . . 'woman radar'.

Silence.

Laura   Oh . . .

Silence.

Danny   I curse it sometimes.

Silence.

Two people could literally be clambering . . .

Laura   Do people honestly . . .

Danny   Like clambering . . .

Laura   Do people honestly clamber?

Danny   You know, to get across the room to get to one another. And I wouldn't notice!

Laura   No.

Silence.

Danny   No radar, see?

Laura   No. No radar.

Laura *retakes her wine and has a drink.*

Danny   I said, honest, I said 'Keith, I'll have the cab back home, you're bang in there'.

Laura 'You're bang in there?'

Danny Yeah!

Laura With who?

Danny With you?

Laura I wanted you, Danny.

Silence.

Danny Oh.

Silence.

Like I said . . . no . . . radar.

Silence.

Laura No, Danny.

Silence.

Danny It's why I've taken up internet dating.

Silence.

That 'Plenty of Fish'. Dear me.

Silence.

At least you know where you stand.

Laura Hardly, Danny.

Danny Have you?

Laura At least if you meet a fella at a bar. Or a party. You can look him in the eye. And make a judgement.

Silence.

Danny Well they either like you or they don't.

Silence.

Laura He's not my friend by the way . . .

Danny Who?

Laura Keith.

Danny No?

Laura He's just someone I know.

Danny Right . . .

Laura He told you we're friends, right?

Danny Yes he did . . .

Laura We're not. I've declined friend requests. On several occasions.

Danny Harsh bitch.

Laura *gives him a look.*

Silence.

Danny Like obviously you're not a harsh bitch, harsh bitch.

Laura I should think not . . .

Danny Like obviously you're not . . .

Laura Well I'm relieved you don't think I'm a harsh bitch.

Silence.

Danny I'm not sure you've got my sense of humour.

Silence.

Keith's a bit of an odd one. A cryptic one.

Laura A bullshitter . . .

Danny Sometimes I just say to him 'spit it out mate'.

Laura A blagger . . .

Danny There's no need to be so fucking spooky, is there?

Laura Like a monumental and bare-faced liar . . .

Danny Laura, I know he's a cunt but he's my mate . . .

Laura Alright.

10 Beginning

Danny Like he's my mate.

Laura And he's a bit of a major wally.

Danny Babe, babe. Since when has someone being a major wally disqualified them from being your best mate?

Laura *laughs.*

Danny Exactly.

Laura To be fair there were quite a few major wally's here tonight. That I've not only accepted friend requests from but I've requested friendships from.

Danny But you'll notice I'm keeping my opinions to myself . . .

Laura You don't like my friends?

Danny Babe . . .

Laura Don't babe me, you don't know me.

Silence.

Danny All I was saying is, is thinking about it, Keith has actually probably got a sort on the go . . .

Laura What are you talking about?

Silence.

Danny It's what I was saying.

Laura About what?

Silence.

Does he even know where his dick is?

Danny Who?

Laura Are you for real?

Danny What?

Laura Keith . . .

Danny Laura . . .

Laura What?

Danny That's who I'm talking about. I know him of old. I know his moods and his moves.

Laura He slept with a girl on my team . . .

Danny I don't understand why he has to hide it. Tell your mates, Keith. Then we all share the joy.

Silence.

With Keith you only find out about it once he's dumped them. Or if he's got the right hump. Because they've dumped him.

Silence.

Laura She quite liked him.

Danny Who?

Laura The girl on my team.

Danny Did she?

Laura She got off with him at our summer party. There was a Bollywood theme and she did look quite nice in a sari. Anyway, he went round to see her on the Sunday and she did a shoulder of lamb.

Danny A shoulder of lamb?

Laura I know. She got it from Budgens.

Silence.

Danny Well he's never once mentioned a shoulder of lamb.

Laura He had the roast, shagged her and then drove home. And then he ignored her texts and calls. She ended up sending him this long embarrassing e-mail.

Danny Shit.

Laura I know, I said don't click and send. But the young ones don't listen to you . . .

Danny No.

Laura She clicked and sent.

Danny That won't go down well with Keith.

Laura Why?

Danny Well he's like a hedgehog in that situation . . .

Laura A hedgehog? A fucking hedgehog?

Danny Well . . .

Laura Within a day she went from feeling a bit shit but essentially being in the right to feeling like a complete tool.

Danny I feel for her . . .

Laura You don't . . .

Danny I know how that feels.

Silence.

They sound quite well suited.

Laura *laughs.*

Laura Like she's got self-esteem issues anyway.

Danny Oh God . . .

Laura And like it compounded them. Massively.

Danny If a bird told me she had self-esteem issues . . .

Laura What?

Danny In the blink of an eye I'd run a fucking mile.

Silence.

Laura To be fair I read the e-mail.

Laura *laughs.*

Beginning 13

Danny Oh, was it cringe?

Laura Oh, it was so cringe. And it made her sound like a lunatic. You know – and she'd been in the right.

Silence.

Danny Oh well, he probably just changed his mind. I would.

Laura Do you have any idea what that does to a woman?

Danny What?

Laura That kind of rejection . . .

Danny Well we've all had a fucking knock back . . .

Laura She was going out of her mind.

Danny Well . . .

Laura What?

Danny I didn't do it.

Laura But he's your mate?

Danny And?

Silence.

She probably overcooked the lamb. He's a bit finicky with his grub is Keith.

Danny *laughs.*

Danny What?

Laura You sexist, patronising, dick. You're as bad as him.

Silence.

Danny Anyway, I'll have another Peroni . . .

Laura If you think I'm opening your bottle for you again you can do one mate . . .

Danny And then I'll get myself a taxi if that's alright, Laura?

Danny *drains away the lager.*

Silence.

He goes to the fridge. It's pretty sparse in the fridge. There's no Peroni but he takes a can of Stella.

He's clumsy and drops it and then without thinking picks it up and opens it. Lager froths out and spills everywhere.

Silence.

Danny Sorry.

Laura I'm getting rid of the carpet anyway.

Danny I am sorry.

Silence.

Laura Don't worry.

Danny I am sorry, Laura.

Laura Forget it.

Danny I'll pay.

Laura Don't be silly. I had the party.

Silence.

I wanted you to stay.

Danny What d'you want me to stay for?

Laura *laughs.*

Laura Don't be a dick.

Silence.

Danny I often think the world would be a better place if people were more modest about their sexual prowess.

Silence.

Laura You often think that?

Danny And?

Laura I often think the world would be a better place if there was peace and no war. If sexual discrimination in the workplace ended. In fact, if there was genuine gender equality and no racism or discrimination of any kind. If children were free from poverty and all kids had a good education. If migrants were welcome. If we got rid of Trident. In fact, if we got rid of all nuclear weapons. If people picked up their litter. If people stopped eating so much red meat. If people were kind and compassionate and considerate and generally nicer. All of those things would make the world a better place. But hey, that's just me.

Silence.

Danny So . . . what like . . . made you want to buy in Crouch End?

Silence.

He drinks. **Laura** *pours more wine. She drinks.*

Silence.

Danny You sure you want me to stay?

Laura Yes.

Danny You sure?

Laura *nods.*

Danny You don't know me?

Laura And?

Silence.

Danny Well I have to say, I was bit, you know, shy about coming to your do.

Laura I told Keith he could bring someone.

Danny I'm only sorry I didn't bring a card.

Laura Don't worry.

Danny It's a bit shit, like coming and not . . .

Silence.

Laura Honestly don't worry.

Danny I did bring a bottle.

Laura I know you did.

Danny It's a lovely flat.

Laura Thanks.

Danny I bet it's not cheap.

Laura No.

Danny You've popped my Crouch End cherry.

Laura A pleasure.

Silence.

Danny *drinks and starts to cough as it's gone down the wrong hole.*

Laura *whacks him on the back. Some lager comes up. He coughs loads.*

Laura You alright?

Danny Fucking wrong hole . . .

Laura *laughs.*

Laura Not the first time I've heard that excuse.

Danny I could have died.

Silence.

The penny drops and **Danny** *blushes and starts to cough again. He composes himself.*

Laura It's only a bit of smut, Danny.

Silence.

Danny I think the Chablis is still in there.

Danny *goes to the fridge and looks.*

Laura Well why don't you open it for me and come and sit next to me?

Silence.

It's a bit sad.

Danny That yoghurt's gonna get up and walk out of there in a minute.

Laura Get the wine and shut the door.

Danny Is that a kiwi fruit?

Laura Probably.

Danny Do you need to refrigerate a kiwi fruit?

Laura I don't know.

Danny My mum has hers in the fruit bowl.

Laura Does she?

Danny She loves a bit of kiwi fruit on her porridge.

Laura Does she?

Danny And a banana.

Laura If you leave that fridge door open much longer everything will go off.

Danny There's nothing to go off!

He does as he's told.

Silence.

You want to look after yourself a bit more.

Laura What?

Danny Get some proper food in.

Laura It's a waste of money on your own . . .

Danny What?

Laura You end up chucking it away . . .

Danny What?

Laura Danny, the wine.

Danny *puts down his can and gets the wine from the fridge.*

He looks around for a bottle opener. He can't find one.

Laura I don't bother with a weekly shop.

Laura *spots one near her and throws it to him, which he catches with his free hand.*

Danny *celebrates the catch.*

Danny Botham style.

Silence.

Laura Was Ian Botham noted for catching the ball?

Danny I'm not really a cricket man.

Laura I assume you're referring to Ian Botham?

Danny Indeed.

Danny *gets to work opening the wine. He breaks the cork as he tries to get it out.*

He struggles trying to get the other half of the cork out but can't.

Laura Just push it in.

Danny *uses an arm of the bottle opener to push the broken cork into the wine.*

Danny *lifts up the wine bottle to inspect it.*

Beginning 19

Danny Sorry.

Laura Don't worry.

Danny I am really sorry.

Laura Stop saying sorry.

Danny I am such a dick.

Laura You are.

Danny Thanks.

Laura No problem.

Danny I'll get my coat.

Laura Don't be a dick.

Danny I know.

Laura Come and sit down next to me and pour me a glass.

Danny *does as he's told. He pours her wine but doesn't sit too near her.*

She drinks.

Silence.

He gets up and goes to retrieve his beer. He looks at the carpet.

Danny I think some cunt's put a fag out on your carpet.

Laura Don't say that word.

Danny Sorry.

Laura I don't mind you swearing. I swear. I just don't like that word.

Danny I'm sorry.

Silence.

Laura Don't be sorry, just don't say it. I don't like it.

Silence.

Danny Yeah my mum loves a kiwi fruit.

Silence.

Laura Don't you want to kiss me?

Danny Well . . .

Laura Don't you want to?

Danny Well I do . . .

Laura Well come and be with me.

Silence.

Danny You're quite forward.

Laura I think you're hot. You're handsome.

Danny Thanks.

Laura I mean it.

Danny Thanks.

Laura I don't believe any of that bollocks about Keith and the taxi.

Danny Oh no, it wasn't bollocks.

Silence.

Laura You honestly couldn't tell I liked you tonight?

Danny I told you. I've got no fucking radar.

Silence.

Laura Alright.

Danny I'm not forward like you.

Silence.

Laura You don't know me.

Danny No, I don't. And you don't know me.

Laura Have you got a problem with a woman being forward?

Danny No.

Silence.

Danny *shakes his head and starts to laugh.*

Silence.

Laura What?

Danny What?

Laura You can't just laugh. And then stop laughing. And not say anything.

Danny What?

Laura You'll make me paranoid.

Danny It was just something silly.

Laura Like what?

Danny Like I was just imagining my Facebook status tomorrow.

Laura What?

Danny Like 'Really hot lady told me I was hot . . .'

Laura 'Really hot lady'?

Danny And?

Laura Fuck's sake.

Danny 'Really hot lady told me I was hot and she wanted to sleep with me last night and I didn't shut the fuck up and I fucked it up.'

Laura What about 'woman'?

Danny What about it?

Laura Woman, Danny, woman.

Silence.

You wouldn't put that on Facebook would you, though?

Danny No!

Laura Would you though?

Danny No!

Laura Over-sharer!

Danny I was just trying to put it out there . . .

Laura What?

Danny The elephant in the room . . .

Laura What?

Danny You know?

Laura I don't know . . .

Danny You know, don't not say what you're thinking . . .

Laura Danny have you got low self-esteem issues?

Danny No.

Silence.

I wouldn't put that on Facebook.

Laura I believe you.

Danny I'm friends on Facebook with my mum and my nan.

Laura You're friends on Facebook with your nan?

Danny She loves it.

Laura Does she though?

Danny She loves a Facebook 'feeling'!

Laura Does she?

Danny Her favourite Facebook 'feeling' is 'blessed'. She's always feeling 'blessed'.

Laura Oh my God, it's like Peter Andre on *Strictly*, do you watch *Strictly*?

Danny Love it . . .

Laura He's always going on about feeling blessed . . .

Danny My mum and my nan both like Peter Andre . . .

Laura I want to meet your nan . . .

Danny Maybe you will . . .

Laura What does your nan say on Facebook?

Danny Well she mostly has rants about the Labour party and makes the odd inappropriate comment . . .

Laura Oh my God, is your nan in the Labour party?

Danny She is . . .

Laura I'm in the Labour party . . .

Danny I'm the apple of her eye and all that, but she thinks I'm a bit Tory boy . . .

Laura She's not racist or anything like that is she?

Danny Course she's not . . .

Laura Oh I didn't mean she was like racist . . .

Danny She's in the Labour party . . .

Laura It's oldies on Facebook, you know?

Silence.

Danny She likes *Downton* and she says things like: 'I'd ride the Earl of Grantham'.

Laura No!

Danny She does and she posts it on my wall!

Laura No!

Danny I don't even like *Downton*!

Laura No way!

Danny It's shit!

Laura How old is your nan?

Danny Ninety-two.

Laura *holds her hand up for a high five.* **Danny** *high fives her and then walks away.*

Silence.

Laura My cousin's a bit embarrassing on Facebook. She's really right-wing. I wasn't being rude about your nan. She sounds amazing.

Silence.

Danny She is.

Silence.

Laura My cousin's a bit racist. Like it's bad enough but you don't want it on your time line, do you?

Silence.

Danny My mum says it's early stages of Alzheimer's . . .

Laura What is?

Danny But it's not.

Laura What?

Danny My nan. I said to my mum 'it's not, if it was early stages of Alzheimer's she wouldn't be able to use the computer'.

Silence.

Laura What about your dad?

Danny Oh he left when I was seven.

Laura Oh.

Silence.

Danny I can't talk about him.

Laura Why?

Danny It's broken my heart my whole life.

His eyes fill up.

Danny So do you like knock on doors and deliver leaflets?

Laura Who for?

Danny I thought you were in the Labour party?

Laura I only joined in August . . .

Danny Oh . . .

Laura I haven't got any time, Danny. And anyway, I can be much more politically active on social media. I mean, I have to be careful. Because I represent my company in those spaces and on those platforms. But still. You're not a Tory are you?

Danny Would it matter if I was?

Laura Because I'm totally with Jeremy.

Silence.

Danny I'm not. I'm not anything. To be honest I don't give a shit about politics. They're all liars. No one's interested in real change. I'm sorry, Laura, I just can't talk about my dad.

Silence.

Laura You alright?

Danny I'm not used to this.

Silence.

Laura Man up.

Silence.

Sorry, that was mean.

Silence.

I am sorry. That was a bit harsh.

Silence.

I think things do get better, Danny. Things will get better. You know this time next year what's going to happen in America?

Danny What?

Laura America is going to elect a woman President for the first time in its history. And then the whole world will know things have moved forwards. For women. For everyone.

Silence.

Danny Shall we just . . . Shall I just call a cab?

Laura No. Don't.

Silence.

Danny She's on Twitter an'all.

Laura Who is?

Danny My nan.

Laura *kills herself laughing.*

Silence.

You're winding me up now.

Danny She is!

Laura She's not!

Danny She is! She does her own hashtag. Nan-tweets.

Laura You're winding me up!

Danny She loves it . . . She gets into spats with Owen Jones and everything.

Laura *looks at him.* **Danny** *starts to laugh.*

Danny Got to admit, I am winding you up.

Laura *laughs.*

Silence.

Laura I bet your profile picture is like, you at the Olympics, or you with a pie . . .

Danny It's not.

Laura No?

Danny It's me and my daughter.

Silence.

Laura Oh right. You're . . .

Danny Yes.

Silence.

Laura Right.

Danny Is that a problem?

Laura No I just didn't . . .

Danny Think I . . .

Laura Yes.

Silence.

What's her name?

Danny Annabel.

Laura That's a nice name.

Danny Thanks. I chose it.

Silence.

Laura How old is she?

Danny Seven.

Danny *takes out his iPhone and shows* **Laura** *a picture of his daughter.*

Laura She's so cute . . .

Danny She's three there . . .

Laura Is that a frog on her jumper?

Danny No it's a rabbit.

Laura Are you sure?

Danny I bought it for her.

Laura Sorry.

Danny Frogs are generally green.

Silence.

Laura Don't you see her?

Danny No. Unfortunately not.

Silence.

Laura I'm sorry.

Silence.

Sometimes I hate Facebook so much. It's like death by Facebook.

Silence.

Danny I know.

Silence.

Laura It's like, if I see another one of my friends, or randoms from Uni, making more cupcakes, or on a trampoline in their huge garden, with their kids . . . I'll like – scream.

Silence.

Danny Even pretend happy families look better than my life most of the time.

Silence.

Laura Does that make me sound bitter?

Danny No.

Laura I sound bitter don't I?

Danny No.

Laura I'm not bitter.

Danny Do I sound bitter?

Laura No.

Silence.

Danny *considers the room.*

Danny You're alright here.

Laura It's nice. Or it will be when it's done.

Danny Do you own this place then?

Laura Yes.

Silence.

Danny Wow.

Silence.

Laura It's only a one-bed.

Danny Still, nice area, Laura.

Laura I like it.

Danny Crouch End . . .

Laura It's great.

Danny Muswell Hill . . . Highgate.

Laura I feel very lucky.

Danny Innit though? It's the pesto triangle.

Laura *laughs.*

Silence.

Laura Do you live in Essex as well then?

Danny Yep.

Silence.

Laura I don't mean to pry.

Danny No, it's fine.

Laura You don't share with Keith?

Danny No, he's an animal.

Laura He is pretty gross when he wants to be.

Danny He sits on the khazi with the bathroom door open and covers up with a copy of *Four Four Two*.

Laura Er, gross.

Danny The man is forty-one years of age. It's no wonder his wife had enough of him.

Laura I never met her.

Silence.

Danny I don't know how Happy puts up with him.

Laura Who's Happy?

Danny Harry, another one of our mates. From school. He's on his own as well, though he doesn't care. That boy does not want for skirt.

Laura For skirt?

Danny What's wrong with that?

Laura Like do you think you're Michael Caine or something? 'Alright geezer . . . Sound as a pound . . . Sound as a pound.'

Danny No.

Laura Like am I 'a nice piece of skirt'? Am I though?

Silence.

Danny No.

Silence.

Laura Well Harry sounds like a right charmer.

Danny Fireman Sam, innit?

Silence.

So Keith's your client, right?

Laura Yes he is.

Silence.

Danny He proper made out that you're friends.

Silence.

Laura We took Keith out for lunch. And we all got a bit trashed. And I said I was having a housewarming. And he sort of invited himself.

Danny That's Keith alright.

Laura He asked me if he could bring a friend.

Danny He bothered to ask then?

Laura I thought it was a bit of a cheek. But I thought what the fuck?

Danny Why not?

Laura New people. All that.

Silence.

So you're divorced?

Danny I am.

Silence.

Laura Recently?

Danny Well obviously not.

Silence.

Laura I don't know, do I?

Silence.

Danny I've not seen Annabel since she was three.

Laura Oh shit. Really?

Silence.

Danny I live back at home with my mum.

Silence.

Laura In Upminster?

Danny Did I . . .?

Laura No Keith . . .

Danny Oh. It's alright. I still like it. I'm really fond of it. It's Upminster Bridge really.

Laura I wouldn't know the difference.

Silence.

Danny I'll get my coat then.

Laura Don't be silly.

Danny Yep well . . .

Laura I really don't give a shit.

Danny Seriously?

Laura I like you.

Silence.

Danny Seriously, I think I will.

Laura You don't meet anyone when you're our age who hasn't got a story.

Danny I feel quite . . . Er . . . Exposed.

Silence.

Laura I've got a story.

Silence.

Obviously nothing like your story.

Danny Thanks.

Silence.

Danny I suppose I've got my baggage. You've got your baggage.

Laura Thanks for that.

Laura *laughs.*

Silence.

Laura Danny?

Danny Yeah.

Laura Hello?

Danny Sorry.

Silence.

Shall we have a bit of a tidy up?

Laura *laughs.*

Danny What?

Laura Come and kiss me. You lemon.

Silence.

Do you like me?

Danny I think you're great.

Laura Do you like me?

Danny I can't relax in here, it's like a bomb's hit it.

Laura What?

Silence.

You've been looking at me all night.

Danny Well, you know . . .

Laura Come and kiss me.

Silence.

Danny Where are the bin bags?

Silence.

Where are they, Laura?

Laura You are such a dick.

Silence.

Danny Let's just have a tidy up. First.

Silence.

Laura They're under the sink.

Danny *goes to the cupboard under the sink and fishes them out.*

Danny You don't get me.

Laura I don't.

Danny I don't just jump into bed with girls.

Silence.

Laura Evidently.

Silence.

Danny Alright?

Laura Okay.

Danny Alright?

Laura Got it. Loud and clear.

Silence.

Danny Like I'm not saying I wouldn't like to.

Laura Thanks.

Danny Like I'm not giving you the brush off.

Laura I get it.

Danny I'm not playing games.

Laura Okay.

Danny I don't play games. I like to be in the mood. Sometimes men like to be in the mood as well.

Laura I tell you what, tidying up's really going to put me in the mood.

Silence.

Well, shall we have a tidy up then or not?

Silence.

Danny You're pretty fit.

Laura Thanks.

Danny I mean it.

Laura Thanks.

Danny I mean I totally would. I mean I totally want to.

Laura Thank you very much kind sir.

Danny I like your hair, Jessie J. It's nice.

Silence.

Like not every bloke is like a dog with two dicks, Laura.

Laura I get it.

Danny Don't get me wrong. I've thought about you. In certain filthy ways in the last half an hour.

Laura Nice.

Silence.

Danny It's been a long time, alright?

Laura Okay.

Danny I like you.

Laura Thanks.

Danny I wouldn't normally ever say this . . .

Laura Say what?

Silence.

Danny To be fair I'm a bit poorly maintained in the area of the groin.

Laura What?

Danny What?

Laura You're poorly maintained in the area of the groin?

Silence.

Danny Fuck's sake.

Laura What?

Danny You know . . .

Laura Danny, I don't know.

Silence.

Danny Put two and two together . . .

Laura I've got no idea what you're talking about . . .

Danny I'm poorly maintained in the area of the groin . . .

Laura What you've got a problem down there?

Danny No!

Laura Well what then?

Danny I can't . . .

Silence.

Laura What?

Danny It's been a long time. Like a really long time.

Silence.

Laura Since you've had sex?

Danny Since I even kissed someone.

Silence.

Laura Is that all?

Danny Oh man.

Silence.

Laura Don't be silly.

Silence.

You know, mate, you need a woman who tells you when to shut the fuck up.

Silence.

Laura *gets up and takes a bin bag from the roll in* **Danny**'s *hands.*

They begin tidying up. They tidy up the rubbish from half the room. It takes the time it takes. Glasses, crockery and cutlery get deposited by the sink. Everything else goes in the bin bag.

They're both dying in the silence. **Danny** *eventually breaks it.*

Danny The sausage rolls were absolutely top drawer, by the way. I thought when I have housewarming for my own place. When I get one again. You know, when I'm with someone.

That's what I'll do. A buffet like that. Salami. Artichokes. Mushroom crostini. But you still need your sausage rolls. Your cheese and pineapple. Class that, Laura. I had three of them. And I love a Scotch egg.

Laura I love a Scotch egg.

Danny Really, it's your favourite?

Laura I have been known to smuggle a Scotch egg out of the pub in my pocket.

Danny I love a Scotch egg.

Laura So do I.

Danny Good. We've got that in common.

Danny *laughs. So does* **Laura**. *They look at each other.*

Silence.

Danny And 'I love a cheeseball.'

Laura 'I love a cheeseball.'

Danny 'I love a cheeseball.'

Laura *laughs hard, getting the reference.*

Laura 'Do you like cheeseballs?'

Danny 'I love a bag of crisps.'

Laura 'Mega.'

Danny 'Love them.'

Laura *laughs.*

Silence.

Laura I see you had a bit of an accident earlier?

Danny Tell me about it. Tomato ketchup's always been my Achilles heel.

Laura What?

Danny When I was a kid my mum always refused to buy me a hot dog.

They continue tidying up until all the dirty washing-up is deposited by the sink and on the work surface and all the rubbish has been bagged up.

Danny My nan always bought me a hot dog.

Laura *gets down on her knees and begins inspecting the carpet.*

Danny It's over there . . .

Laura What is?

Danny The fag burn.

Laura *heads where he's pointing.*

Laura Fuck.

Danny Where are the marigolds?

Laura What?

Danny Well I don't want to just go rifling through your drawers, Laura.

Laura *stands up.*

Laura Danny, it's really lovely and you're really lovely . . .

Silence.

Danny It won't take long.

Laura But I have to say I've got a strange ominous feeling that I'm not going to get laid tonight.

Silence.

Danny Don't say that.

Silence.

Laura It's very sweet, Danny.

Silence.

You are very sweet.

Silence.

We can do the washing-up in the morning. Or I can do it when you've gone home.

Silence.

It doesn't matter.

Silence.

Can you relax now?

He nods and glances at some housewarming gifts and cards.

Danny Nice teapot.

Laura *goes and sits on the sofa.* **Danny** *washes out a wine glass and pours himself some Chablis.*

Laura *lifts her glass.* **Danny** *fills it.*

Danny Aren't you pissed?

Laura I've drunk myself sober.

Danny *wanders over to the armchair and sits in it.*

Silence.

Laura I'm not like this with every guy.

Silence.

Danny Up to you what you do.

Silence.

Laura I don't generally jump on men. I mean, you're not exactly the best candidate to be jumped on are you?

Danny Thanks, babe.

Silence.

Like I say.

Laura What?

Silence.

I'm not like that.

Silence.

I was with someone for ten years. I was though.

Silence.

I've been on my own for the last couple of years.

Silence.

Danny What, you've not had a bit for a couple of years either?

Laura No.

Danny What no you have, or no you haven't?

Laura I have had sex. Of course I have.

Silence.

Danny Oh.

Laura Is that a problem?

Danny No. Good luck to you.

Laura Good luck to me?

Silence.

Danny I hope you've had loads because I've had fuck all.

Silence.

The most I can say is I've had a long tortured unrequited love affair with Aliona off *Strictly*.

Laura You like her?

Silence.

Danny I mean, you've got to admit she's hot.

Laura *shakes her head and really laughs. A bit too hard.*

Silence.

Danny *picks something out of his teeth and inspects it.*

Laura　Danny . . . Er, gross.

Danny　Fucking cork, innit.

Silence.

Danny　Me and Aliona in St. Petersburg. Me and Aliona in Barbados. Me and Aliona in Disneyland with Annabel.

Silence.

Laura　Jay's hot.

Danny　He's so dull.

Laura　He's not. He's got a bit of reserve. A bit of mystery.

Danny　Dull. As. Dishwater. A grey man.

Laura　You're just jealous.

Danny　Damn right I am.

Laura *laughs.*

Silence.

Laura　We can watch *Strictly* in bed in the morning if you want?

Silence.

We can watch it on iPlayer.

Silence.

Danny　Have you had a look in your bedroom?

Laura　Why?

Danny　That girl with the hair fell asleep on your bed with a pint of red wine. And she had a little puke as well. And then she woke up and scarpered.

Laura *bolts out of chair and then stops herself.*

Laura Fuck it.

Danny Keith told me.

Laura Great.

Danny One of your other mates took pictures and she FB'd it. It looked quite funny actually. She already had thirty-five likes after about three minutes.

Silence.

Laura *looks at* **Danny** *and decides to go back to the sofa.*

She drinks.

Laura Well Keith obviously thought it best to warn you in advance.

Danny Hum.

Laura Considerate.

Danny Suppose so.

Silence.

Who was that girl with the hair?

Laura I work with her.

Danny She's a bit eccentric.

Laura She's alright.

Danny She thinks she's fucking Paloma Faith.

Silence.

Laura Why don't you see your daughter?

Silence.

Why do you live with your mum?

Silence.

Laura I got pregnant. When I was first with my ex.

Danny Did you?

Laura I didn't keep it. I felt like I was too young at the time.

Silence.

I've only ever told my girlfriends that.

Silence.

Danny Darling, I am your black cab driver for the night.

Laura *laughs.*

Silence.

Danny Did your ex know?

Laura I wish he didn't.

Silence.

Danny It's a nice flat this flat.

Silence.

Laura It's my third flat. Don't you know, I was Mrs Sensible and bought when I was twenty-three.

Silence.

Danny Did you buy with your ex?

Laura No, he was Australian.

Danny You know some of those Aussies do actually like settle down and buy property . . .

Laura He moved in with me.

Danny And did he earn his crust?

Laura Why are you saying that?

Silence.

Danny Sorry.

Laura He worked in a bar and did a bit of general handyman stuff.

Silence.

I had an ex-local authority place in Kentish Town and then I sold that. And then I bought a flat in Archway. Although it was mine and I pretty much paid for everything I couldn't stay there after we split up. But I couldn't quite give it up. Until now. I couldn't quite give up Waterlow Park. Does that sound silly though?

Danny The hardest thing I ever did in my life was walk out of my home.

Silence.

Laura Will you stay tomorrow?

Danny What?

Laura Don't get up and go tomorrow morning.

Danny Alright.

Silence.

You might want me to.

Laura I won't.

Danny Why?

Laura I can tell.

Danny I might be a shit fuck.

Laura Danny.

Danny What?

Laura I hate Sunday on my own.

Silence.

I can't bear another Sunday on my own with a hangover.

Silence.

You want to go now, don't you?

Danny No.

Laura You do though, don't you?

Danny No.

Laura You've changed your opinion of me.

Danny No.

Laura I can see it all over your face though, Danny.

Danny I haven't.

Laura You think I'm needy now.

Silence.

Danny I don't.

Silence.

I'll have to give my mum a bell.

Silence.

Laura What?

Silence.

Danny In the morning. Otherwise she'll fret. And then Mum'll be on the phone to Nan. And then Nan will be posting embarrassing messages on my Facebook. And then they'll both think you're a nightmare. Before they've even met you.

Silence.

Laura Oh you're going to introduce me to your family are you?

Silence.

Danny I might do. If you play your cards right.

Silence.

Laura Oh, if I play my cards right?

Silence.

Danny Do you believe in love at first sight?

Silence.

Laura Yes.

Silence.

Danny *gets up.*

Laura Talk to me. Properly.

Silence.

Danny You're too good for me.

Silence.

Laura Even to fuck me?

Danny I only fuck girls I might want to be with.

Laura No one only fucks people they might want to be with.

Silence.

Danny It's what you want, innit though?

Laura What?

Danny To be treated as a person.

Laura Yes I do . . .

Danny Not as an object.

Silence.

I've got a daughter.

Silence.

Laura Why are you emasculating yourself?

Silence.

My life's a shell of activity.

Silence.

My parents are both dead. I've got no brothers or sisters.

Silence.

I've got money. Not a fortune, not now. But some.

Silence.

I look out in life. I look up. I look at the sky. I like to walk up to Ally Pally on a Sunday.

Silence.

If I looked in, I'd fold inside myself.

Silence.

I'm ovulating.

Silence.

Danny You're what?

Laura I can feel I'm ovulating. I always know. I can feel it.

The penny drops. **Danny** *understands what she's saying.*

Silence.

Laura You don't know what it's like.

Silence.

All I'll ever be is 'Auntie Laura'.

Silence.

Danny So I'm the spunk?

Silence.

Laura No, I really like you.

Danny You don't know me from Adam.

Silence.

Laura My dad always said you can't go far wrong if you just put your hands up and tell the truth.

Silence.

Danny Well thanks for being honest.

Silence.

I couldn't take my eyes off you all night tonight.

Laura I know.

Silence.

Danny It's hard to trust though, innit?

Laura Maybe.

Danny When you've been hurt.

Silence.

This is all taking me some guts, Laura.

Silence.

Laura And me.

Silence.

Danny Is it though?

Laura I've been trying to find the courage to be with you all night.

Silence.

Danny D'you think I'm a prick?

Laura No.

Silence.

You returned my gaze.

Silence.

It doesn't define who I am. It just doesn't. I've done all sorts of things in my life Danny. But it is what I want now.

Silence.

Danny Well I have to say, babe, I've spent all day on a Saturday, when I could have been over West Ham, in a room full of suits in Milton Keynes. I was looking forward to a few beers tonight. But it's turned out a bit different than I expected in the end.

Silence.

Have you ever been to Milton Keynes?

Laura No.

Danny Don't bother.

Silence.

Laura What were you doing there?

Danny Recruitment Consultancy Expo two thousand and fifteen. I can tell you, it was a hoot.

Silence.

Laura It's like sometimes, everything you say is another obstacle. Another dare not to like you.

Danny What, sometimes or everything I say?

Laura Don't be like that.

Danny I'm sorry. I . . .

Silence.

Laura 'If I say this, will she still like me now? If I do this, will she still like me?'

Silence.

I like football.

Danny Really?

Laura I went with my dad.

Danny To the fucking Arsenal I bet.

Laura To Millwall.

Danny No! No! You didn't!

Laura *laughs.*

Danny No! Laura! No!

Laura Fished in.

Silence.

Danny I wish I'd met you online.

Laura Why?

Danny Because everything would be so much easier.

Silence.

Laura And how is internet dating going for you?

Danny 'How was', you mean.

Silence.

I couldn't stand my loneliness. I couldn't stand their loneliness. They all wanted kids. Some of them were more up front about it than others. But it was always the same.

Silence.

The loneliness. The patency of it.

Laura Patency?

Silence.

You like to rough up your edges, don't you?

Danny I don't know what you mean.

Laura Play the boy.

Danny Not really.

Laura I bet you went to Uni and did English or something like that?

Silence.

Danny Where did you go to Uni?

Laura In London. In Mile End.

Silence.

Danny What did you do?

Laura English.

Danny I did History.

Laura Where?

Danny Bristol.

Silence.

I'll never be able to afford a flat like this.

Laura You don't know that.

Silence.

Danny What did you give for it?

Laura Does it matter?

Danny Four-fifty? Five hundred grand?

Laura Something like that.

Danny You must have a good job though?

Laura I'm the MD of the agency where I work.

Silence.

Danny You're MD?

Laura Yes. I'm the Managing Director.

Silence.

Danny What d'you want with someone like me?

Silence.

You wouldn't look twice at me online.

Laura I haven't met you online.

Danny Oh, I forgot, you want my spunk.

Silence.

Awkward.

Laura A bit.

Danny Shall we put some music on?

Laura Why not?

Danny The people downstairs won't mind?

Laura They're away.

Danny Cool.

Laura Hence tonight.

Danny *goes to the iPod dock and collects the iPod. He has a look through.*

Danny I liked your playlist.

Laura D'you want anything in particular?

Danny I'm easy.

Laura Just stick it on shuffle.

Danny *puts the iPod back in the dock, finds the party playlist and presses shuffle.*

'Lady (Hear Me Tonight)' by Modjo plays. It's very loud so he turns it down.

The song plays on. **Danny** *speaks up over it.*

Danny Tune.

Danny *makes a very awkward effort to dance. So does* **Laura** *on the other side of the room.*

The song plays to its end.

'I Owe You Nothing' by Bros plays.

Laura *is delighted and sings along and begins to dance as she sings. She's quite flamboyant. She encourages* **Danny** *to dance with her, but he won't.*

The song finishes.

'We No Speak Americano' by Yolanda Be Cool & DCUP plays.

They listen to the song.

Two-thirds through it she gets up and switches it off.

Silence.

Laura So . . . You didn't feel like dancing?

Silence.

Have you got any coke?

Danny No, don't do it. Have you?

Laura No, don't really do it.

Silence.

I think you should just go home.

Danny Did you plan this?

Laura No.

Danny You said Keith could bring a friend.

Laura I got the idea tonight.

Silence.

Danny And you expect me to believe that?

Laura It's the truth.

Danny I don't know, Laur . . .

Laura I wanted to be near you and I just thought . . .

Danny What?

Laura Fuck it.

Silence.

Danny Fuck it?

Laura My daddy called me 'Laur'.

Silence.

Danny Have you done this before?

Laura No.

Silence.

Danny And you expect me to take that on trust?

Laura I'm thirty-eight years old and I've been sensible my whole life, Danny.

Silence.

Yep I did, I thought 'fuck it, fuck him and see what happens'. I know another woman that's done it. And. And. I like you. You've got a nice face. A kind face. You're nice, I can tell. I want my baby to have a nice daddy.

Silence.

You know, I'm quite capable of getting myself down to a Harley Street sperm bank. If I'd wanted to. Let's forget it.

Silence.

Danny What's your favourite bit?

Laura Of what?

Danny The sausage meat and breadcrumbs – or the egg?

Laura Oh.

Danny What's your favourite bit?

Laura Egg.

Danny Runny or hard?

Laura Hard.

Danny Motorway service station dirty Ginsters or Jamie?

Laura Dirty Ginsters every time.

Danny Love a bit of Jamie myself. You ever made one?

Laura No.

Danny It's worth it.

Laura Is it?

Danny Nice bit of pickle on the side.

Laura Gastropub wanker.

Danny You love it.

Laura All you need is HP sauce.

Silence.

Danny D'you cook?

Laura Oh fuck off. D'you want to know if I do the ironing as well?

Silence.

Danny I didn't mean anything by it.

Silence.

It's hard at Mum's because the kitchen's not mine, but I try to cook.

Laura Personally, I find Jamie Oliver a bit of a tosser.

Danny You can't knock Jamie.

Laura Why?

Danny I remember watching *The Naked Chef*. I used to love it. I used to dream of having a scooter and knocking up some tucker for me mates like him.

Laura That's sweet.

Danny I like cooking. Genuinely, Laura. When I was married we had a massive kitchen.

Silence.

Laura I can cook for us tomorrow.

Silence.

It's been a long time since I cooked for a man.

Silence.

I can go out for eggs and bacon and a paper.

Silence.

And I can get some stuff in for lunch and dinner.

Silence.

It's been so long since I've done that on a Sunday.

Silence.

Danny I can cook.

Silence.

Laura Let me.

Danny I don't know though.

Silence.

I don't know about staying.

Silence.

Laura Get us out of the hole, Danny.

Silence.

I only wanted to be honest.

Silence.

Danny Nothing's even happened between us.

Laura You think nothing's happened?

Silence.

I've put my heart in my hand and I've shown you it. Offered it. Freely.

Silence.

I've been brave.

Silence.

How brave are you, big man?

Danny How stupid d'you think I am, you mean . . .

Silence.

You know after everything I've been through you think I'd . . .

Laura I wouldn't know because you haven't told me.

Danny Well you know it's only been an hour, hour-and-a-half and I'm just about getting my head around what's in your head.

Silence.

I don't know you.

Laura How many times in your life have you connected with someone like this?

Danny You think we've connected?

Silence.

I do think you're different. To women I meet. Generally.

Silence.

I do find you attractive. You can see I do.

Silence.

Maybe I'll fuck you later. If that's what you want. Maybe I won't.

Laura I don't want you to fuck me. You fucking twat.

Silence.

Danny I could kill for something to eat. Have you got a slice of toast or anything I can have?

Silence.

Laura Are you hungry?

Danny I'm hanked, Laur.

Silence.

Laura D'you want a fish finger sandwich?

Danny Do I want a fish finger sandwich?

Laura Yeah.

Danny That's honestly a question though?

Laura Do you though?

Danny Hello – earth calling Laura, mister ketchup stain is in the building.

Laura *laughs.*

Danny I'd love one, babe.

Silence.

Laura *gets some frozen fish fingers from the freezer and then fishes some baking trays out of her oven.*

She takes one tray and arranges six fish fingers on the tray. She switches on the oven and puts the fish fingers straight in.

Danny Fan assisted. Nice.

Silence.

Laura I know it's a cardinal sin when you're buying to get sucked in to the fixtures and fittings as per. But I loved this oven and they said they'd leave it.

Laura *goes to the fridge and takes out some ketchup and mayonnaise.*

Silence.

Laura *notices* **Danny** *looking at her.*

Danny I'd go a Ginsters with you.

Laura I'd go a Ginsters with you too.

Silence.

Danny 'Crouch Endy' were they?

Laura Journalists. Very Crouch End. Like old-school Crouch End. When I first had a look round she was on her way out with their son to 'Bongo Babies'.

Danny *laughs.*

Laura I know. He was a sweet boy.

Danny How old was he?

Laura About ten months.

Danny It's when they start to get fun.

Laura Called Dashiell.

Danny Oh why did they do that?

Laura What?

Danny You've got to pass the playground test . . .

Laura What?

Danny He'll get bullied.

Laura Not round here he won't. It's a cute name.

Danny What they staying round here then?

Laura No.

Danny Well then . . .

Laura I said 'After Hammett?'

Danny What?

Laura They said they just liked the name. But she took great pleasure in telling me Cate Blanchett had called her son Dashiell.

Danny Oh what a wanker. Honestly, though?

Silence.

Laura He called him 'Dash' and she called him 'Dashy'.

Danny I mean, that's quite sweet innit?

Laura I mentioned *The Incredibles* but they didn't get it and they made a point of telling me 'Dashiell doesn't watch TV'.

Danny God, they sound awful.

Laura I thought, I bet the fucking nanny sticks a DVD on when they've gone to work.

Danny They've got a nanny?

Laura Yep.

Danny God.

Laura Even if I had that kind of money I wouldn't want a nanny for my baby.

Silence.

Danny Annabel loved *The Incredibles*.

Silence.

Laura I was the wanker though.

Silence.

Dashiell took a shine to me and I asked them if I could have a cuddle.

Silence.

It was completely inappropriate but I was offering asking price.

Silence.

It was so wonderful.

Silence.

Danny You weren't a wanker. You're not a wanker.

Laura They've bought a house in Mill Hill. I wouldn't want a nanny. I wouldn't want my kids educated privately. It's nice to have the choice. But you have to make the right choice.

Danny We're the lucky ones.

Silence.

Laura I've only been in here six weeks and it already feels like an admission of defeat.

I kept thinking, why buy a two-bed in an area I don't like when I can live in Crouchy . . .

Danny At least you've got your own place. I'd send my kids to private school. I'd scrape the fees for Annabel if it meant I could see her. You do the best for your kids, don't you?

Silence.

Danny *goes to the bread bin and takes out a loaf of sliced white bread.*

He takes the butter dish and finds a knife and begins to butter four slices.

Silence.

Danny You will meet someone.

Laura It's not like that when you're our age . . .

Danny You will have a baby.

Laura Danny, that's just blind optimism.

Danny You will. If it's what you really want.

Silence.

Laura If that was the case I'd be married by now, with three kids and in a big house in East Finchley.

Silence.

I definitely wouldn't be making five people redundant on Monday morning. We don't call them redundancies any more. We call it 'simplification'. I don't know whether it's kind or the most ludicrous and monstrous thing I've ever heard in my life.

Silence.

Danny You didn't know you wanted it until you realised you might never have it.

Silence.

Laura I don't want a mirror, Danny.

Silence.

You're wrong anyway. It's something I've always wanted really. Even when I was younger.

Silence.

Danny *casually looks at some mail on top of the microwave.*

Danny Miss Laura R Eggleston?

Laura That's me.

Danny What's the R for?

Laura Rose.

Danny Laura Rose Eggleston. You're posh, innit?

Laura Hardly though.

Danny Were you 'Eggy' at school?

Laura Yeah. And 'The Ston' in sixth form.

Danny My mates call me 'Julius'.

Laura Julius?

Danny No one can remember why.

Laura *laughs.*

Danny A bloke at work – his nickname's 'Spunk Bubble'.

Laura Why?

Danny His mum and dad had a split condom.

Laura Er, gross.

Danny Don't you think it's funny though?

Laura Fancy his parents telling him that?

Danny And the little shit's proud of it as well.

Laura Is he? What a dick . . .

Danny Perhaps we should christen our one . . .

Silence.

Laura What?

Laura *looks at* **Danny.** *They look at each other, examine each other.*

Danny *goes and sits down.*

Silence.

Danny I would do it you know. Part of me's like – fuck it though.

Laura That's like how I feel.

Danny I fancy you rotten.

Silence.

But I could do it and I could have a fucking brilliant day with you tomorrow like.

Laura I think we would, you know?

Danny And we could do it again tomorrow.

Laura I think we click, genuinely.

Danny And then you could never want to see me again.

Silence.

And nine months down the road there'd be me and two kids of mine I never see.

Silence.

I don't think my heart could take that.

Laura I was honest with you because I like you and I can see you're a good man.

Danny You don't know me.

Silence.

Laura It probably wouldn't happen anyway . . .

Danny I'm not stupid . . .

Laura I know you're not.

Danny What's the chance, one in ten? One in twenty?

Silence.

Laura You know if you did . . . And I did . . . I would never do that.

Danny What?

Laura You know . . .

Danny What?

Laura I would never exclude you.

Danny That's what my ex-wife said.

Silence.

It's crazy we're even having the conversation. It's fucking nuts.

Silence.

Laura Who knows what's going to happen?

Danny I fucking wish you'd kept your mouth shut and said nothing and just fucked me.

Laura No Danny . . .

Danny And held me and told me nothing and given me an amazing night tonight and day tomorrow.

Laura Danny . . .

Danny I need someone to hold me as well. You think a man doesn't need that?

Laura I never said that . . .

Danny You think a man doesn't need warmth and love?

Laura I know, I need it . . .

Danny Why couldn't you just give me that and give yourself that?

Laura I wanted to . . .

Danny And deal with your guilt . . .

Laura Danny, I can't use someone like that.

Silence.

Danny You think you're the only one that's lonely?

Silence.

I thought nothing could be lonelier than an unhappy marriage. But I tell you it's got nothing on sitting there with your mum and your nan on a Monday night after work. And you've got absolutely nothing to say to each other though.

Nothing. And you're forty-two years of age. And all you can think of is your daughter you've not seen for four years. And what happened at school that day. And whether she's going to dancing classes or learning to play the violin. And you go up to your room. The room that was your room when you were a kid. And it's still got the claret and blue on the walls. And you see the toy box in the corner. That was your toy box when you was a kid. Except now it's full of your daughter's toys from. Four years ago though. Peppa Pig and, and . . .

Silence.

And you haven't got a clue what she's into now. Or whether she even remembers you. And knows she's got a dad. Your own flesh and blood.

Silence.

Your whole life's gone. Everything you were certain of. It's gone.

Silence.

I'd top myself if I knew it wouldn't devastate my mum and my nan. I'd do it though.

Silence.

I'm not even a shell, babe. I'm candy-floss an hour out of the maker.

Silence.

When the train was coming in to take us back to Euston this afternoon. I went there. In my head.

Silence.

And I looked at those idiots that I work with. And I thought, I won't give you a fucking story that'll be an office joke within a week.

Laura Fucking hell, Danny. If you're gonna do it, don't do it in Milton Keynes.

Danny *starts to laugh. He wants to cry but he doesn't let himself cry in front of* **Laura**.

Silence.

Danny   You make me laugh.

Silence.

Laura   You'd never do anything like that.

Danny   No, I wouldn't.

Laura   I can tell.

Danny   I worry I'll never see Annabel again.

Silence.

Laura   It must be lonely.

Danny   It is.

Laura   It must be a lonely thing to live with?

Danny   You frighten me. They way you look at me. You unpeel me.

Silence.

It makes me think about the man I was.

Silence.

I'm the bloke in the park on a Sunday morning. Having a fag. Watching every other dad with their kids. What's wrong with you, Laura? You can't just decide things like this on a whim . . .

Laura *screams.*

Laura   You think I want a baby on a whim!

Silence.

Danny   I'm sorry.

Silence.

Laura Don't worry.

Danny I'm sorry, Laura.

Laura *goes to the oven and takes out the fish fingers.*

She makes two fish finger sandwiches and puts lots of ketchup and mayonnaise on both of them.

She gives **Danny** *his sandwich and then returns and collects hers.*

She eats hers. He doesn't touch his. She finishes her sandwich.

Laura Why don't you see Annabel?

Danny Because she lives in Truro now.

Laura Then get a lawyer.

Danny I've got no money left. She's gone back to Cornwall.

Silence.

Her mother does what she likes. She's so much like me. Annabel. She's the spit of me.

Silence.

I'm a monthly direct debit. That's all I am.

Silence.

Danny *lights up a cigarette and smokes.*

Silence.

Laura We moved here when I was thirteen. When Mum met Dad. And we lived on Landseer Road. I was there until I went to Uni. It was just me and Mum and Dad. He was always my dad. I took his name when Mum did. My dad was a postman and my mum was a teacher. We were a unit.

Silence.

My mum got ovarian cancer when I was twenty and she was dead six months later.

Silence.

It was awful. But in a way it was a lot worse seeing what happened to Dad, though. He was always a modest drinker. Half of ale, half of bitter. But when Mum went Dad drank.

Silence.

He drank a lot. He smoked. He smoked all the time when she was gone. I think he found it hard to be around me. He said I'm so much like Mum. He was dead within three years.

Silence.

I was amazed he managed to hold down his job until he died.

Silence.

He left me some money. There wasn't much. He'd not been paying the mortgage. He was a law unto himself once Mum had gone. You couldn't tell him anything. Is that you?

Silence.

Danny　No, Laur.

Silence.

Laura　I don't need a man. I don't need you. Not really.

Silence.

I'm not desperate for a man. I'm quite happy on my own.

Silence.

Eat your sandwich, Danny.

Danny *does as he's told and eats his sandwich. He stops and looks at her.*

Danny　How would it work then?

Laura　What?

Danny　If we go to bed.

Laura　Er, I don't know about my bed.

Danny　The sofa then.

Silence.

Laura We'd just do it.

Danny And?

Laura And we'd cuddle up and go to sleep.

Danny And what then?

Laura And then we'd do it again in the morning.

Danny And what after that?

Laura I'd go out to get breakfast, like I said I would.

Danny And you'd see me again?

Silence.

Laura I don't know. I think I would. I honestly don't know. I can't say any more than I've said to persuade you. It's not right. I don't know, Danny.

Silence.

Danny All I've ever wanted is to be is a family man.

Laura I can see that.

Silence.

Danny Do you promise me if I do what you want and if it happens and you know . . . You . . . You'll always include me?

Silence.

Laura They'd always know their dad.

Silence.

Danny Do you promise me you'd always include me?

Laura I can't make that promise, Danny. I don't know you.

Silence.

You don't have to do anything you don't want to do. I've been completely up front with you.

Silence.

Danny But Annabel?

Laura What about her?

Danny She'd have a brother or a sister . . .

Laura I can't help you with your ex.

Silence.

Danny So it's your call? It's going to be your call . . .

Laura Yeah, I think it is.

Silence.

Danny So it's a punt?

Silence.

Laura Or maybe the beginning of something.

Silence.

Why did you split up with your wife?

Danny We stopped listening to each other.

Silence.

Laura And that ended a marriage?

Silence.

Danny We stopped talking to each other.

Laura That's sad.

Danny We had Annabel. A home. But we didn't have each other. We had Annabel but we forgot everything else we had in common.

Silence.

Laura That is sad.

Danny Yep.

Laura Especially for Annabel.

Silence.

Danny I had an affair.

Silence.

Laura I did wonder.

Silence.

Danny It was . . .

Laura What?

Danny I don't know.

Silence.

Laura D'you have regrets?

Silence.

Danny I don't know if I can talk to you about this yet.

Silence.

Laura That's fine.

Danny You get it though, right?

Laura Of course I do.

Silence.

Are you still in love with her?

Danny Who?

Silence.

My wife?

Laura Well, I guess . . .

Danny No . . .

Laura I meant . . .

Danny Her?

Laura I guess so – yes. The woman who . . .

Danny No, no, I'm not.

Silence.

Laura I mean, it's none of my business.

Danny It's fine.

Laura It isn't though.

Danny I don't mind you asking . . .

Laura Really . . .

Danny As long as you don't mind if I don't want to talk about it.

Silence.

Laura Of course I don't.

Danny I feel ashamed.

Laura Oh don't . . .

Danny I feel I let myself down . . .

Laura No . . .

Danny And I feel like I let Annabel down.

Laura Don't though.

Danny It's true. I'm not a bad man.

Silence.

Laura If you knew everything about my life you wouldn't like me.

Silence.

Danny I don't think there's a person in this world you could say any different about.

Silence.

I don't care what your past is.

Silence.

I care about now. The now. It's all I care about, Laura. How d'you want to live your life now? What d'you want to do now?

Laura You know.

Silence.

Danny Tell me what you want.

Laura You know what I want.

Danny Tell me about what happens next.

Silence.

Laura You walk towards me and kiss me.

Danny I kiss you.

Laura We kiss like it's the kiss that makes you feel like you're home.

Silence.

You take my hand and we sit next to each other. With ease, though.

Danny With ease?

Laura And we kiss again. You undress me.

Silence.

Everything apart from my knickers. And you kiss me as you undress me. My eyelids, my neck, my shoulders, my breasts, my tummy. But you don't touch me. Not yet. You kiss my thighs, my calves, my heel, my little toe. And then you rise.

Silence.

And I undress you. Slowly. Carefully. Kissing. Just kissing. You let me touch you.

Silence.

Danny It's been a while . . .

Laura I know . . .

Danny I think you might be better off letting me get in there.

Laura *laughs.*

Danny *lights a cigarette. He thinks. He puts it out.*

Silence.

Laura We fall asleep on the sofa for a bit. We get up and turn the mattress over on my bed and change the bedding and we sleep. You know about tomorrow. But tomorrow night. Sunday night. When it's time for you to go. You say you're staying. You ring your mum. And she rings your nan.

Danny *laughs.*

And you tell her that you're not coming home.

Silence.

We get the W7 to Finsbury Park and kiss each other goodbye at King's Cross, when you get off. But you go and buy a clean shirt and some deodorant though. And then you go to work. And I go to work. And as I walk up Tottenham Court Road I think about you. And I dream.

Silence.

I dream like I haven't dreamt in years.

Silence.

Of coming home and you coming home to me, and me to you. And I'll know in my heart I'll never be lonely again.

Silence.

No more giving everything to work. Because already life is beginning.

Silence.

In a year this place is sold and there's me and you and . . .

Laura *wants to cry. She won't cry in front of him.*

Silence.

No more in the gym at seven. No more foreign films on my own and a meal deal for one. No more reading every book on the Booker shortlist and making smug recommendations to Tuesday Book Club. No more just 'Auntie Laura'. None of it.

Silence.

What's wrong with that?

Silence.

What's wrong with wanting to have a family and be married and be normal though?

Silence.

My friends are all so jealous of my independence. My career. My courage embracing being on my own. My travelling. My dates, my lovers, my embarrassing nights out.

Laura *screams.*

But it's so, so, so . . . You know?

Danny *nods.*

Silence.

Laura   I want a people carrier. I want a big house in Essex. I want kids. I want a family. I want a husband. I want to work from nine till five Monday to Thursday and then have the day on a Friday to be with my son or my daughter. I want to be married. And I want a normal husband I can rely on. And I still want a fucking white dress. And I want to put all the pictures on Facebook. Every last single one, though. I want pictures of you kissing me on the steps of the church. Of you dancing with me to Bros. Of you carrying me up to our room when I'm totalled at the end of the night. I want pictures of me with your mum and your nan. Who both love me. I want pictures of us with our baby. I want pictures of me making cupcakes with him. Or her. Or him. Or her. I want the place on the Amalfi coast. I want to be a size fourteen. I want us to go to the opera and you to wear black tie. Just because we've never done anything like it before and maybe we'll never do it again because we hate it. But we'll laugh. We'll laugh ourselves sick with laughing. We'll turn fifty and start looking the same. Me with short hair. And us in matching body warmers. And we'll cruise. We'll go on a cruise just like my mum and dad did. Before they died.

Silence.

But we won't die young like them. We'll be like the couple I saw at Heathrow.

Silence.

Eighty, maybe ninety. Him in a jacket and trousers. And her in a long elegant violet dress. Holding hands. Holding hands and never letting go.

Silence.

Danny   I'll never be able to give you that.

Laura   I know.

Silence.

Danny   I've got nothing.

Silence.

Laura   I know.

Silence.

Danny   You need a man who can give you the life you want.

Laura   I don't want a cunt with an Audi.

Silence.

I want The You. I want The You. That's what I want.

Silence.

Danny *goes to her and kisses her. They kiss.*

Danny *takes her hand and leads her to the sofa.*

They kiss again.

Danny *begins to undress her. Slowly, kissing as he goes. Until she's just in her bra and knickers.*

Laura *kisses him and removes his shirt. She kisses as she goes.*

Laura *undoes his belt.* **Danny** *stands and his trousers fall.*

Danny *moves away slightly and takes off his socks.* **Laura** *stands.*

They both look at each other in their underwear.

Silence.

Danny I'm sorry about my . . .

Laura What?

Danny My belly.

Silence.

Laura You'd do this?

Danny I don't want to talk any more.

Silence.

Laura I'm scared now.

Danny Don't be scared.

Laura I am.

Danny Don't be.

Laura I feel like my whole life's on the toss of a coin.

Silence.

Laura *thinks, makes a decision and goes to find her handbag. It takes a while, but she finds it.*

She roots around inside and takes out her purse. She fishes out a condom.

She offers it to **Danny**.

Danny Right.

Laura I want to though.

Danny Laur . . .

Laura Laura.

Danny I'm cool with it.

Laura If you still like me. And I still like you. In the morning then we can . . .

Danny I am cool with it . . .

Laura I've only got this one anyway.

Silence.

Something changed when you came tonight. And you looked at me.

Silence.

Danny Same.

Laura I know.

Silence.

I've got to trust that though.

Danny I get it, babe.

Silence.

Is there any chance you can flick the heating on?

Laura What?

Danny I feel like the last chicken in Sainsbury's.

Laura *really laughs.*

Silence.

Laura *goes to* **Danny** *and holds him. They just hold each other.*

Laura You getting warmer?

Danny Not yet.

Laura Just give it a minute.

Silence.

Danny If you tell me where the thermostat is though . . .

Laura *lets him go, goes to the dial on the wall and turns up the heating.*

She stays where she is and looks at him.

Laura You don't think this is crazy?

Danny No.

Laura You sure?

Danny When has anyone ever got it on with anyone and it's not felt crazy?

Silence.

Like even a tiny bit.

Silence.

Laura I think you're amazing doing this.

Danny Why?

Laura When I put my cards on the table I was expecting you to just walk out.

Danny Why would I automatically do that?

Laura I don't know, I . . .

Silence.

Danny Laura, you're the brave one.

Laura I'm trying to be.

Laura *smiles.*

You're absolutely sure?

Danny Yeah.

Laura We're good people. You and me. Come here.

Silence.

I want a good beginning.

Danny *nods.* **Laura** *advances towards* **Danny** *and they kiss.* **Danny** *takes her hand and leads her towards the sofa.*

He takes the condom from her and looks at it. He thinks, makes a decision and places the condom gently to one side. They kiss.

Fade. The End.

Middle

For Bertie, Wilf & George

Middle had its premiere in the Dorfman Theatre at the National Theatre, London, on 4 May 2022 with the following cast and creative team:

Maggie	**Claire Rushbrook**
Gary	**Daniel Ryan**
Director	Polly Findlay
Set and Costume Designer	Fly Davis
Lighting Designer	Rick Fisher
Sound Designer	Donato Wharton
Movement Director	Anna Morrissey
Fight Director	Bret Yount
Voice and Dialect Coach	Nia Lynn
Staff Director	Lucy Jane Atkinson

Late February, 2016.

The large kitchen of a detached house in Shenfield, Essex.

It's big enough to comfortably home a kitchen island with bar stool-type chairs. It's spotlessly organised and clean but you can tell a child, or children, live in this house from some artwork on the fridge door.

The kitchen is mostly modern but there is a sideboard with glass cupboard doors containing their large collection of fine bone china tableware and dinnerware. Most stuff is put away, leaving clean surfaces and lines. But there's a knife block. A bluetooth speaker. And a fruit bowl with bananas, some satsumas and a couple of kiwi fruit.

It's neither night, nor morning, some time after four. The only light is coming from the cooker hood and a lamp.

Maggie, *49, pours some milk into a saucepan and heats it on the hob. She does it carefully, slowly, she doesn't want to burn the milk, minding her dressing gown sleeves. She glances briefly at her iPhone and then puts it in her dressing gown pocket.*

In the kitchen doorway is her husband, **Gary**, *49, in West Ham United pyjamas. He sips water that he brought down with him.*

Gary *watches his wife pour the milk into her M mug. She takes a sip. She finally looks at him.*

They look at each other for a long time, for as long as you think you can get away with.

Gary   Didn't you want to use the microwave?

Maggie   No.

Gary   It's a lot easier.

Maggie   I didn't want to.

Gary   Two minutes. Bing.

Silence.

Maggie I can never get it just how I want it.

Silence.

Gary Or put it on for a minute. Stick your finger in. Twenty more seconds. Thirty more seconds. Job done. Bosh.

Silence.

Maggie I would have thought a microwave's more of a 'Bing' than a 'Bosh'?

Maggie *smiles, sips.*

Silence.

Gary *comes further into the kitchen and slips his iPhone from his pyjama shorts pocket and looks at something, then scrolls for a moment. Then he plugs it into a charger plugged into the wall.*

Silence.

Gary What's wrong?

Silence.

Maggie I can't sleep. I haven't been to sleep at all.

Silence.

Gary What's wrong?

Silence.

Maggie I'm not sure I love you anymore.

Gary *blinks and fetches the kettle, which he fills and then flicks on.*

He fetches his G mug and another fresh mug for **Maggie***.*

He fetches the teapot from the sideboard. He watches the kettle boil. The kettle boils.

Gary Oh. You don't want any tea do you?

Maggie No.

He looks at her, composes himself. She looks at him, holds his gaze.

Silence.

Gary What?

Silence.

Maggie Did you hear what I said?

Silence.

Gary You know what? We didn't defrost the pork.

Gary *goes to the freezer and takes out a frozen pork belly.*

I knew when we went to bed we'd forgotten something.

He finds a plate and puts the pork on it.

Maggie Gary, did you hear what I said?

Gary I know I'm in trouble when I'm 'Gary'.

Gary *goes back to the mugs and teapot and throws in two teabags. He re-boils the kettle, pours water into the teapot. He looks at her.*

What?

Maggie Gary?

Gary I can't believe you woke me up again.

Silence.

I was having a really good sleep. I was in a really deep sleep. I was having a wonderful dream.

Silence.

I was in a big holiday camp. At a school reunion. Like that Butlin's at Minehead. But more old-fashioned, like *Hi-De-Hi*. There was cod, chips and mushy peas for breakfast. All over that. And they was all there from school. But everyone had gone grey. Like exaggerated. Lucy Wilson looked like she had a silver wig on. And she was the fittest girl in my year. Adam Phillips had brought along the model he did of the Thames Barrier. As his Geography project. And everyone said he was still a muppet. And Michael Keeley was taking pictures on a proper camera. We went on the flumes. Played on the penny pushers. Everyone tried to crack on with Lucy Wilson like they did at school.

And she kept winking at me. But I ignored her. Everyone was dancing to 'So Macho'. By Sinitta. And we was all having a right laugh. Hands in the air. Like you just don't care.

Maggie I wish I had your dreams.

Silence.

There's never any point to them.

Gary They're just dreams.

Maggie I wish mine were like that.

Silence.

What was the one the other day?

Gary I dunno.

Maggie The one about the fish?

Gary The fishing one, the one at the fish counter in Sainsbury's, or the one about the funny smell in the lift at work?

Maggie What's the one about the funny smell in the lift at work?

Gary Didn't I tell you that one?

Maggie What's that one?

Gary It was an odd one. I had this dream. Just before I woke up. I was in the lift at work. And I went up in it. But I was on edge. And I didn't know why. I thought I could smell fish. So I didn't get out at my floor. And I went down again. And I went up and down about ten times. I was so on edge. I thought, I swear on my life I can smell haddock. I can really smell haddock. Then there was a horrendous noise. I thought I was having a heart attack! The alarm went off!

Maggie The fire alarm?

Gary No, my alarm! My real alarm! Did my nut right in. It was like I was in a hundred-piece puzzle. With eighty-two of the pieces missing. And to make it worse when I got in the actual lift at work. Like, the real, actual lift. It didn't smell of anything! And I even asked Johnny Cartwright if he could smell anything. And he looked at me, like I'd confirmed once and for all I'm a liability. Everyone thinks I'm a liability at my firm.

Maggie *smiles and nods.*

Silence.

Maggie I suppose that's the difference between real life and a dream. One's real and one's not.

Until it all starts to merge into the same thing.

Silence.

Gary So what was the one the other day about the fish?

Maggie Gary . . .

Gary Was it the one about the humongous carp?

Maggie I want to talk . . .

Gary Was it that one?

Maggie I've not slept for weeks.

Gary Just tell me . . .

Silence.

I know what this is all about. It was the same with me mum.

Silence.

Maggie What?

Gary The painters are no longer in very often. And in fact they're packing up. And they've nearly left the building.

Silence.

Maggie It's not that.

Silence.

You think this is about that?

Gary *moves as if in response to something he can hear upstairs.*

Gary That's Annabelle.

Maggie It's not.

Gary It is. That's Annabelle.

Maggie It's the radiator. At the top of the stairs.

Gary It's not.

Maggie The heating's come on.

Gary Are you cold?

Maggie No. Are you?

Gary I'm alright.

Maggie Why don't you go and put your hoodie on?

Gary I'm alright.

Maggie You're cold, I can see you're cold.

Gary I don't want to.

Silence.

Maggie She's never up in the night. You know she's not.

Silence.

She's not been up in the night since she was in Reception.

Gary I was just saying . . .

Maggie Why don't you go and get your hoodie and have a peek in?

Gary I'm fine.

Maggie You'll reassure yourself.

Gary I'm alright as it is.

Maggie Go on.

Gary I don't want to.

Maggie I don't want you to be cold.

Gary It'll warm up.

Maggie I don't want you to worry.

Gary I know, it's the radiator.

Maggie I want us to talk. I don't want you to keep diverting off.

Gary I'm not.

Maggie You are.

Gary People say stuff when they're married. Truly awful terrible things. Things they don't mean.

Maggie Gary . . .

Gary I have . . .

Maggie Gary.

Gary I've said things to you . . .

Maggie Babe . . .

Gary That argument we had on holiday still brings me out in a cold sweat . . .

Maggie Gary, we don't need to go over it . . .

Gary What's with all the 'Gary'?

Maggie I just called you babe . . .

Gary Gary this, Gary that. Gary, Gary, Gary.

Silence.

Maggie Please. I want you to listen to me.

Gary I am, I swear.

Maggie I want you to pay attention.

Gary I'm all ears.

Maggie This is important.

Gary I know, babe.

Maggie Please help me.

Gary I want to.

Maggie Help me to do this well.

Gary Okay, okay . . .

Maggie I've wanted us to talk for weeks and weeks and weeks . . .

Gary I'm all ears, honest . . .

Maggie But since Friday . . .

Gary What happened Friday?

Maggie *cracks a touch, wipes away a couple of tears. Holds it together.*

Gary *goes to her, tries to hold her but she doesn't want him to. She pushes him away.*

Silence.

Gary Mag . . . Honest, I'm all ears.

Maggie *looks at him.*

Silence.

Gary's *a little at a loss. He sips the water he brought down with him. He notices the pork belly on the plate.*

Gary What d'you think about sprinkling a few fennel seeds on that pork?

Maggie What?

Gary I had a little looky-see on tinterweb last night. And this one recipe reckons a rub. Fennel seeds, some chopped rosemary and lemon zest. With the seasoning and . . . Have we got any fennel seeds?

Maggie I've no idea.

Gary *looks about him, wanders a bit in the kitchen.*

Silence.

Gary I love it in here. I love it, I just love it. Get the tunes going. The Roses, the Mondays, bit of Pulp. Bit of eighties. Bit of Prince. An Old School Banger. An Indie Banger. Bit of Luther. Bit of Otis.

Silence.

Rattle a few saucepans. Cook up a storm. You and me and Annabelle having a nice early dinner. A spag-bol. A nice authentic one. Having a laugh.

Maggie I know.

Silence.

Gary You know if you're not up to Mum and Dad . . .

Maggie I'm not sure I am . . .

Gary I mean we made such a song and dance. About saying thank you for last weekend . . . And Annabelle's gonna be like: 'What's happened to Nanny and Grandad?'

Maggie I don't even know where I'm gonna be in the next ten minutes. Let alone this afternoon.

Silence.

Gary D'you want a brandy?

Maggie No.

Gary You sure?

Maggie Yep.

Gary I think there's a Bailey's left over from Christmas . . .

Maggie I don't want a drink.

Gary It might help . . .

Maggie It won't . . .

Gary I might still have that spliff that Spam Face gave me on my forty-fifth. I think it's in me pant drawer . . .

Maggie Gary . . .

Gary Might be a bit . . .

Gary smacks his lips and waggles his tongue.

Maggie I don't want to drink, I don't want to get stoned. I want to talk.

Silence.

Gary Alright.

Silence.

We had a lovely Valentine's weekend away. Lovely. Didn't we? Lovely pub, lovely grub, nice walk on the beach. Lovely room. Sex twice. Twice.

Maggie I know.

Silence.

Gary It was great to get away on our own.

Silence.

Maggie I didn't want to.

Gary Go away?

Maggie Have sex with you.

Silence.

Gary Mag? What you saying, Mag?

Maggie I haven't wanted to have sex with you for ages.

Silence.

But I've done it. I've done it. I have done. I read up, I talk to people, I'm not stupid.

Things change. Things can change. But you think of your marriage. Get the lube out. 'It's like having a biscuit. Once you've had one, you feel like another one.' Why do you think I've done it? Why d'you think we did it twice?

Maggie *wipes away a few tears, then composes herself.*

Silence.

Gary Don't you fancy me no more?

Silence.

Maggie I wish we were healthier. But I'm the same. It's hard working up town. How many times have I tried to have that conversation with you, Gary?

Silence.

Maggie I think there's things we could have done.

Silence.

Gary Annabelle's school fees ain't gonna pay for themselves, are they Mag? I ain't gonna be able to do what we need to driving an Uber, am I?

Maggie Sending her to Brentwood Prep was your choice.

Silence.

Gary Look, I feel gutted right.

Maggie I'm sorry.

Silence.

Gary It's gonna go up and down, ain't it babe?

Maggie What is?

Gary We've had our ups and downs. Like everyone.

Maggie What are you talking about Gary?

Gary You know, the fancying. Even when you've hit the jackpot and married an Adonis like me.

Gary *makes a few shapes to try and make* **Maggie** *laugh. He has no luck.*

Silence.

Maggie Gary . . .

Gary We ain't had no time for ourselves for donkeys' years. Listen to me . . .

Maggie No, Gary, listen to me . . . Please.

Gary My opinion on this, right. You've got to tackle these things. Head on. You've almost got to have a hit list . . . In the sack.

Maggie No Gary . . .

Gary Stay with me, babe.

Maggie No, I don't want to . . .

Gary I think with the sex thing. There's bits and bobs we can do . . .

Maggie Bits and bobs?

Gary Yeah.

Hearing him talk like this is very hard for her.

Silence.

C'mon! We can jazz things up!

Maggie *looks at the clock on the wall, nearer five than four now.*

Gary When it comes to the bedroom department, I may not always be Uri Geller. But I have on occasion unwittingly stumbled upon your internet history. Forgive me. But who am I to quibble, if two big hairy coppers with leather chaps and a multifunctional truncheon are forming a queue at Mrs Maggie's Wank Bank?

Gary *holds his hands up.*

Maggie No Gary, I . . .

Gary I ain't never gonna be the most hirsute fella, babe. But as for the attire. They do, do next day delivery at 'Love Your Leather dot co dot UK'.

Gary *smiles.*

We've all got fantasies. I have. I can tell you. I'm in a black cab. Going down a country lane on a hot summer's day. I'm sweaty. And my driver. She's sweaty. If you want me to paint a picture. She's like Carol Kirkwood's younger sister. Just less smiley. Almost sullen. Like she needs me to take her away from all this. And I can just see a little bit of boob . . . In the rear view mirror. And I'm like 'hello soldier'. And I say to her 'you look like you need cheering up darling'.

Maggie *puts her head in her hands.*

Silence.

Gary I bought you a vibrator.

Maggie You didn't, did you?

Gary Surprise!

Silence.

Well I wanted it to be a surprise. I was gonna bring it last weekend. But you kept coming in when I was packing my bag. And then Annabelle was in and out with her iPad.

Maggie Oh God . . .

Gary I wanted you to feel nice. I was nervous.

Silence.

And like I wanted you to know. I didn't take you for granted. And I was really cacking my pants buying it. I put me Peaky Blinder on and me Ray-Bans on when I went in Ann Summers in Romford.

Maggie *covers her mouth with her hands, eyes still closed, finding courage.*

Gary I reckon I went in and out of there about ten times before I had the nerve to pick one up. And I didn't know whether you might want like a cool midget-type one. Or a great big donger . . .

Maggie Gary . . .

Silence.

Gary In the end I just bought one of each. Fuck it.

Silence.

The big lad's a nine-inch throbbing veined monster. Made with hospital-grade silicone. I've hid him in the loft. He's in with the Christmas decorations.

Silence.

Maggie I don't love you any more. I doesn't how much you talk and talk and talk. I don't love you any more.

Gary Stop it.

Silence.

Maggie I don't love you any more.

Gary Stop it.

Maggie I don't, I don't love you any more.

Gary Stop it.

Maggie I don't love you any more.

Gary Mag, darling . . .

Maggie I don't love you any more.

Gary Mag . . .

Maggie I wanted to talk to you. But I knew it would be like this. I'm just going to go upstairs and get a few things and go to Mum's. I don't want a scene with Annabelle. You can make up whatever excuse you like. And perhaps once you're in the frame of mind to talk. Then we can talk.

Gary blinks away a tear, cut to the core.

Silence.

Maggie Are you crying?

Gary No.

Maggie I don't mind.

Gary I'm not.

They look at each other for a long time, for as long as you think you can get away with.

Maggie Do you want a brandy?

Gary No.

Maggie It might help.

Gary I'm alright.

Maggie Limoncello?

Gary I don't think now's the moment for a limoncello.

Maggie Go on.

Gary I tend to associate a limoncello with a nice meal at Tarantino's.

Silence.

Or the lovely holiday we had in Italy.

Silence.

Maggie Why don't you have a brandy?

Gary I can't . . .

Maggie Why not?

Gary I've got to take Annabelle football.

Maggie Not until nine . . .

Gary No . . .

Maggie Maybe she won't go football tomorrow for once . . .

Gary It's already today.

Maggie Maybe she won't go football today . . .

Gary No she's not missing it . . .

Maggie Why not?

Gary Why don't you love me no more?

Silence.

Maggie I do. As a friend.

Gary As a friend?

Silence.

Sixteen years and I'm in the friend zone?

Silence.

Why don't you love me no more?

Silence.

Maggie We are friends . . . And we're family. And we're parents . . .

Gary Like, I know you're more intelligent than me . . .

Maggie Don't say that . . .

Gary You are . . .

Maggie Well I'm not . . .

Gary But I'm not thick.

Maggie I know you're not.

Gary Brian next door. Now he's thick . . .

Maggie What's this got to do with Brian?

Gary I'm not thick . . .

Maggie I know you're not.

Gary Then when I ask you a straight question why won't you answer it?

Silence.

Maggie Because I'm frightened. I'm petrified.

Gary Of me?

Maggie No.

Gary What?

Maggie Can't you understand why I'm scared?

Gary You're scared? And how d'you think I'm feeling right now?

Silence.

I've only got up for a piss. And you're insomniac again. Up and down. Rolling over this way, rolling over that way. Crying.

Maggie If you knew I was crying why didn't you say something?

Gary Why do you think?

Maggie Why didn't you give me a cuddle?

Gary Because I'm shitting myself that's why! I'm frightened half to death!

Silence.

Maggie I honestly don't know where to start.

Gary You've already started.

Maggie It's hard.

Maggie *walks in the kitchen, trying to be composed and find courage.*

Silence.

I'm so bored.

Silence.

I feel so lonely.

Silence.

I'm so sorry to hurt you like this Gary.

Maggie *wants to cry but maintains her composure.* **Gary** *is devastated.*

Silence.

Maggie Let me try and do this as best I can.

Silence.

Remember when we first met? It was the first Friday back after Millennium Eve, right?

Gary I know when it was.

Maggie In 'Hamilton Hall'.

Gary I know where it was.

Maggie There's something I never told you.

Silence.

I bumped into my ex.

Gary In 'Hamilton Hall'?

Maggie On Bishopsgate.

Gary Outside the pub?

Maggie Outside 'The Woodins Shades'.

Gary You said . . .

Maggie I know what I said.

Gary You said you just fancied a drink before you got on the train?

Maggie I did.

Gary You didn't do anything did you?

Maggie What d'you mean?

Gary With him . . .

Maggie Like what?

Gary Before you met me?

Maggie I bumped into him on the street outside 'The Woodins Shades'!

Silence.

Gary Well what then?

Silence.

Maggie He told me it was biggest mistake of his life letting me go. He had tears in his eyes. He was always a man who had tears in his eyes when he needed them.

Silence.

And as he waved his hands about. Declaring his love and asking me for my new number. I was crying. Because he hurt me so much. And deep down I still loved him. And I thought about him. And then I could see it glinting. His wedding ring. Waving his hands about, he was. 'I love you Maggie, I love you'. And it meant nothing more to him than a tinsel end in the gutter.

Silence.

Gary Your ex was married?

Silence.

Why didn't you tell me?

Maggie It didn't affect you . . .

Gary Didn't it?

Maggie I walked away from him. And I walked away from every shit-bag City Boy I ever knew. With the gift of the gab, a pair of loafers and two nights a week in a titty bar. And you was there. You was at the bar.

Maggie *closes her eyes.*

Silence.

When we got together it was complicated for me . . .

Gary It wasn't complicated for me . . .

Maggie I was heartbroken and you fixed me.

Silence.

They were golden times. Our honeymoon in Krabi was like a dream. I'll remember the day we spent in Phang Nga Bay until the day I die. I've never had such a laugh. I've never felt so safe with a bloke. They were golden times. They were. It was such a good time.

We were always having a laugh. And we had such nice sex. Sexy sex.

Silence.

When you asked me to marry you I knew it was me and you forever. I knew.

Gary Why don't you love me any more?

Silence.

Maggie You made me want things I never wanted before. I wanted a big house on the Mount. I wanted big holidays. Dubai. The Maldives. Tahiti. I wanted a family.

Gary I know you wasn't sure about having Annabelle . . .

Maggie That's not true . . .

Gary Be honest.

Maggie I find Annabelle difficult.

Gary She's alright.

Maggie Well maybe you think she's alright because she's not difficult with you.

Gary She can be.

Maggie She's always been Daddy's girl.

Silence.

I was stuck with her all the time.

Gary Stuck with her?

Maggie That's how it felt.

Silence.

Gary You know there's women who'd be grateful to be in that position . . .

Maggie I know. But I'm me. And I wanted a year out. Max.

Silence.

Gary We was gonna try for another one.

Maggie I didn't want to have another one.

Gary But you promised me we'd try for another one.

Maggie No Gary, I promised to keep an open mind . . .

Gary Well maybe we should have had a shag once in a while. Or you should have kept our appointment . . .

Maggie I was all over the place . . . I'm sorry.

Gary And I was up and down Harley Street like some wally who'd gone to the wrong clinic . . .

Maggie I'm sorry, I've said I'm sorry a hundred times.

Silence.

I didn't always have luck with men. But I had a great life. And then I spent five years on my own.

Gary Don't be silly . . .

Maggie I'm not. Five years on my own . . .

Gary You weren't on your own . . .

Maggie You're out the door at six every morning. You're out up town three nights a week. Your clients tell you to bend over, you bend over. I mean who goes on a client's stag do?

You're playing golf, you're over West Ham . . . You're forty-nine years of age. Where's it all going to end? When you drop down dead of a heart attack?

Silence.

My mum told me, when you have a kid you just have to accept your relationship plateaus for a while. Or it goes backwards. Well there's that and there's your marriage falling off of Beachy Head. Except when it's smashed to bits on the rocks. It refuses to die. It's just stuck there, bored and tired and lonely. Trying to attract some attention. Someone. Anyone. Help me. The tide goes in, the tide goes out. Still there. No one notices, no one cares. Bleeding to death for eternity.

Silence.

Gary Everyone finds having a kid hard.

Maggie There's hard and there's hard . . .

Gary Things have been fine since you've been back at work . . .

Maggie Things have been, tolerable. That's not the same . . .

Gary Come on Mag, what is this bullshit?

Maggie Believe you me, I've been circumspect. I'll tell you another thing you didn't know. If you didn't let me go back to work when Annabelle started school I was going.

Gary Let you go back to work?

Maggie You heard me . . .

Gary You do as you please, babe . . .

Maggie You heard me . . .

Gary Going where?

Maggie I was leaving.

Gary Well perhaps you should have done and saved yourself another three years of misery with me?

Maggie I often wish I did.

Gary *paces, this is all so hard.*

Silence.

Maggie You have no idea how patient I've been.

Gary Why are you bringing all this shit up from years ago?

Silence.

I don't want this.

Maggie I didn't want us to argue . . .

Gary I love you.

Silence.

Maggie I wanted to talk. And explain how I feel in an honest, calm, way. I've been going over it and over it in my mind.

Silence.

Gary And what about my feelings? Don't I have feelings? Or am I just the geezer?

Maggie I'm sorry I've hurt you . . . I am.

Gary Hurt me? You've cut me in half.

Silence.

Maggie I've always thought about you.

Gary Have you?

Maggie When I first met you it was complicated. Of course, I thought about whether I was being fair. Of course, I felt guilty. Like I was carrying around unfinished business. But I really liked you. And I fell in love with you.

Silence.

It was right giving things between us a chance. I was so happy. Those years were great. I loved our wedding. Loved it. All the dancing. The eighties theme. The silly dancing. To Yazz. And Bros. And Wham.

Silence.

I never dreamed it would take so long to have Annabelle. I just didn't.

Silence.

I always thought it would be so smooth. I was so terrified by my mum growing up. Use contraception or you'll get pregnant. So obviously I thought as soon as we start trying it'll happen.

Silence.

Like I know how normal losing a pregnancy is now. Losing a baby. A little baby. Can be. But it wasn't normal to me. It was devastating. It happening. And then again. And the IVF not working out. That was really hard. Depressing. And. Like it made me feel we weren't meant to be. Somehow. Like on some deep level of fate. It completely doomed us.

Silence.

And when I fell pregnant with Annabelle I . . . And it just happened. Naturally. Like it was supposed to all along. It wasn't just like it was a miracle. It was confirmation. Like we were alright with the world. We were meant to be.

Silence.

I was so ecstatic I . . . I was like. This is our dream. This is our dream come true. This is it. And then when she was here.

Gary She was a miracle.

Silence.

Maggie You had a fortnight off work. And it was a blur. I can't really remember it. And then you went back to work. And I was on my own.

Silence.

I spent a lot of time feeling guilty. Not at first. But once we were married and trying to have a family.

Silence.

I felt like I was letting you down. Letting Annabelle down.

Silence.

And when I couldn't breastfeed I felt like a complete failure. I felt worse than you can possibly imagine. I don't think we ever talked about it once. Not even once.

Silence.

And when you went back to work. Annabelle was two weeks old. I was so scared, and so lonely and isolated . . .

Gary You had your mates . . .

Maggie Thank God. Thank God.

Silence.

Five years of mums. Mum-ness. I've written the book, got the badge. There's not a children's entertainer in Essex I'm not on first-name terms with. Awesome Andrew sends me a personalised e-Christmas Card . . .

Gary Who's he?

Maggie Did the kite-flying party for Annabelle's fourth birthday. In Weald Park. I advised Jill at Stay and Play on improving her range of healthy snacks. For children. And adults. I made and consumed every possible variety and concoction of cupcake. My chocolate and salted caramel ones with a Rolo were a hit for two years running. And my pistachio with hand-crafted mermaid tails were spectacular.

Silence.

Yeah I had my mates. To laugh and cry with. Thank God. But I needed you.

Silence.

I love being a mum. I love it. It's hard, it's fucking hard. But I was so much more than that. I am so much more than that. A mum. And a wife.

Silence.

Believe me, I've been circumspect. Rattling around in a big empty house. It's been better in the last few years since I've been back to work but . . .

Silence.

I really appreciate everything you do for us. I really do. But what about me?

Silence.

You wanted another one. But I always had two children to look after.

Silence.

I reckon you're right. I reckon I'm perimenopausal. I've been to the doctor.

Silence.

I know I'm getting on. And as I'm thinking about getting older. I'm frightened.

Silence.

The thought of us being together. Getting old together. It used to make me feel so safe.

Gary *starts to wipe away a few tears.*

Silence.

Maggie I'm sorry.

Gary What for?

Maggie Let me get you a tissue . . .

Gary I don't need a tissue.

Maggie Gary . . .

Gary I told you Mag. That floor cleaner you use in here makes my eyes itch. When Annabelle makes a mess use the Mr Muscle Five-in-One.

Silence.

Why are you doing this?

Silence.

Funnily enough five years of endometriosis and my below-par sperm count wasn't on my bucket list. But you wanted to be at home with Annabelle . . .

Maggie Not forever.

Gary It wasn't forever . . .

Maggie It felt like it. I didn't want everything to be on my shoulders . . .

Gary You've got a short memory . . .

Maggie I didn't put my hand up for that.

Gary Tell me what to do.

Maggie What?

Gary Tell me what to do. To put things right.

Maggie Gary . . .

Gary I love you Mag. I've loved you since the minute I set eyes on you.

Maggie Gary, please . . .

Gary You know it's true.

Maggie Please, just let's talk.

Gary You tell me what to do and I'll do it, babe.

Silence.

I thought all this was water well under the bridge. As it goes, since Annabelle started school. And you went back to work. I thought things had been great. I think things have been weird. Like lately. I thought you was a bit quiet over Christmas. And off like a rocket. But I thought, she's just starting to go through the change. We had such a lovely Valentine's last weekend. Didn't we?

Silence.

When you told me you didn't want another kid. And you wanted to go back to work. I was gutted. But I accepted it. And I did what you want. Because that's what you do, right? When you're married and you love someone. Right? But that's three years ago now darling. We're plodding along. Annabelle's thriving. We have a couple of nice holidays a year. We get out. Maybe not as often we should. But we get a nice date night. My lot help out. Or your lot. Annabelle's getting bigger. Perhaps we should have more nights away.

Gary *studies her.*

Silence.

You tell me. Tell me what you want and I'll do it. I promise you.

Maggie *thinks, finds courage, walks in the kitchen.* **Gary** *watches her.*

Silence.

Maggie   I think I'm in love with someone else.

Gary *is shattered.*

Silence.

Maggie   I'm sorry. I'm so sorry.

Silence.

Gary   Who? Is it your ex?

Maggie   Gary . . .

Gary   Is he back on the scene?

Maggie   No.

Silence.

Gary   Is it Martin?

Maggie   No, of course it's not.

Gary   Who is it?

Maggie   It's not Martin. It's no one at work.

Silence.

Gary   Who is it then?

Silence.

Maggie   His name's John.

Gary   John?

Maggie Yeah.

Gary I don't know any John.

Maggie I know you don't.

Gary There's John down the road. But he's eighty-two and he's deaf as a post.

Silence.

Maggie You don't know him.

Silence.

Gary You've been having an affair?

Maggie I haven't slept with him.

Silence.

Gary You haven't shagged him?

Maggie No.

Gary I don't understand this.

Silence.

Maggie I feel so awful.

Gary You haven't shagged him?

Maggie No.

Gary I don't . . .

Maggie But when I saw him on Friday . . .

Gary On Friday?

Maggie At lunchtime.

Gary Lunchtime?

Maggie We meet for a Pret. Or sometimes YO! Sushi!

Gary YO! Sushi!

Maggie Yeah.

Gary I thought you didn't like sushi?

Maggie Well you know . . . I've given it a go.

Silence.

When I saw John on Friday we kissed.

Gary You kissed another man?

Maggie Passionately.

Gary *weeps a bit, wipes away a few tears, holds it together.*

Silence.

Maggie And I felt like a Rubicon had been crossed.

Silence.

I'm sorry I've hurt you . . .

Gary I'm alright . . .

Maggie Let me get you some kitchen roll . . .

Gary I've told you already, I'm not crying . . .

Maggie You don't have to pretend to . . .

Gary If I was crying don't you think I'd know about it?

Silence.

Maggie Okay Gary, alright.

Gary John?

Maggie Yeah.

Gary What's John do then?

Maggie He's a policeman.

Gary *sits down and puts his head in his hands.*

Silence.

Maggie He's not like a uniformed policeman. He hasn't got a truncheon. They were phased out in the mid-nineties.

John explained. Like, I have seen a picture of him in his dress uniform. When he was younger. But he's a detective. You know Brian next door has actually got criminal associations. John's in Homocide and major Crime Command. He's a very impressive man.

Silence.

I met him in the pub. Much like I met you.

Silence.

Gary Is John married as well?

Maggie It's on its last legs.

Gary What is?

Maggie His marriage.

Gary Right.

Maggie He's not loved his wife for years.

Silence.

He's been a very good friend over the last three months.

Gary Three months?

Silence.

Maggie I won't lie. We've both felt tempted. But we've kept each other on the straight and narrow.

Silence.

Gary So what's been going on?

Maggie It's all been very innocent.

Gary It doesn't sound innocent to me?

Maggie I feel so shit.

Silence.

Gary Don't you think you owe me an explanation?

Maggie *nods.*

Silence.

Gary You met him in a pub?

Maggie Yeah.

Gary Where?

Maggie Does it matter?

Gary Before Christmas?

Maggie More like November.

Silence.

I met him in Dirty Dicks.

Gary Dirty Dicks?

Maggie On Bishopsgate.

Gary I am familiar with the establishment.

Maggie Alright.

Gary Was it that leaving do? Was it? Ella's leaving do?

Maggie *nods.*

Silence.

Maggie He chatted me up at the bar.

Gary Chatted you up?

Maggie Well not chatted up, chatted up . . . It wasn't like that. He told me all about his wife. And his kids.

Gary He's got kids as well has he?

Maggie He was just being friendly. I told you. It was all very innocent.

Silence.

He found me on Facebook . . .

Gary He's not on your Facebook is he?

Maggie No!

Gary Our whole life's on Facebook!

Silence.

Maggie It's not, Gary, is it?

Silence.

I've kept him completely out of our life.

Silence.

We just struck up a private friendship. He's having a really hard time. I feel so sorry for him. His eldest daughter from his first marriage is anorexic and his wife's got an over-active thyroid.

Silence.

I was lonely. I am lonely. You've got no idea. I can't sleep. I'm awake. I know you're awake as well. Neither of us is saying nothing. And sometimes my heart. It's like it hurts so much. It's so swollen. Like it could burst. And then, then. It's like it's being squeezed. And squeezed. Like it's in the grip of something terrible. And unyielding. And I feel like I can hardly breathe.

Silence.

It's got a hold of me night and day. Night and day. Night time is worst. I never dreamed in all my life my marriage bed could be so lonely.

Silence.

It's taken me a long time to realise how lonely I've been, Gary. Because you to tend to think. When people say they're lonely. You tend to think of solitude. Of being on your own. But it's a different kind of loneliness. All the things you want to say but you can't. The sadness of it. The disappointment.

Silence.

I know this is selfish. After everything I've said. But all I want you to do is cuddle me in the night. And kiss my ear. And tell me you'll look after me.

Silence.

But it's not fair is it.

Silence.

We've got a lot in common.

Gary Thank you.

Maggie I meant me and John.

Silence.

We come from very similar backgrounds. He's from Royal Tunbridge Wells. His dad was a civil servant and his mum was a teacher. Well she's gone now but. And he went to university. And he got a job up town. He was a graduate in the Bank of England.

But a desk job didn't suit him at all. And so he became a copper. He's like me. He's very interested in current affairs. And whatnot.

Silence.

And you know he says he likes nothing more. Nothing more. Than to listen to Classic FM and read a book. He reads everything that's on the shortlist for the William Hill Sports Book of the Year.

Silence.

And I think I'd like that. Instead of coming in and sticking the telly on. Whatever Annabelle's watching on Netflix. Or whatever you're watching on Sky Sports News. Listen to the radio. And read a book.

Silence.

I grew up in a house where Radio Four was always on. When I was younger I always had my nose in a book. I don't know where she's gone.

Silence.

Or perhaps we could talk. Actually talk to each other.

Gary I thought we did.

Maggie We don't talk. We give each other instructions. We make arrangements.

Silence.

John's been a very good friend. Very good. When we meet up for a drink. Or a coffee. Or to go to an exhibition.

Gary You've been to an exhibition with him?

Maggie To the Tate Modern. I told you I've been wanting to go for ages.

Gary No you didn't.

Silence.

Maggie We talk. We talk and talk and talk and talk and talk and talk and talk.

Silence.

I can't stop thinking about him.

Silence.

I just can't. From the minute I open my eyes. When I made the tea yesterday morning I imagined making him tea. He likes it weak. I think it looks like cat's piss. But it's how he likes it. When I had my shower I thought about him . . . I.

Silence.

Until the minute I finally decided to come down. And make myself a drink. That's what it's been like. Since Friday. Since he give me a late Valentine's card. And he finally took my hand. And I let him kiss me.

Gary *stands.*

Gary You've made him tea?

Silence.

You've had him haven't you? You're bullshitting me, this is all shit . . .

Maggie I haven't. I promise you. He came here one morning. When I had the day off to go to Thaxted. With Annabelle's school.

Gary What, so that was all lies?

Maggie It wasn't till the afternoon.

Silence.

John was impressed with your golf clubs.

Gary He what?

Maggie He liked your Sand Iron.

Gary He what?

Maggie He pulled it out and had a swing.

Gary He had a swing with my Sand Iron?

Silence.

Maggie John wanted to kiss me.

Gary You've brought this man into my home?

Maggie But I lost my nerve.

Gary You was gonna have some fucking bloke in our bed?

Maggie No . . .

Gary Oh one of the guest bedrooms. That's alright then.

Maggie No Gary I wasn't.

Gary Well what was he here for then?

Maggie I meant my marriage vows, Gary.

Maggie *lifts her left hand almost defiantly.* **Gary** *looks at her, her wedding ring. She lets her hand fall.*

Silence.

Maggie I've been thinking about when I met you a lot. I've not slept a wink. We was only thirty-three then.

Silence.

I wanted security. I wanted someone nice for a change. And you was there.

Silence.

Sometimes I think I don't deserve you, Annabelle. All this. And sometimes I think I settled for someone and something I never should have. In a million years.

Maggie *studies* **Gary.**

Silence.

Maggie I want to be completely honest. That's all.

Gary *opens the sideboard cupboard doors and methodically smashes every single piece of tableware and dinnerware in there on the kitchen floor. It takes as long as it takes.*

Finally, he comes across a surviving milk jug. He looks at it and then throws it as hard as he can across the room, **Maggie** *ducks, and it smashes against the opposite wall.*

Silence.

Gary You know what . . .

Maggie What?

Gary It's overrated . . .

Maggie What is?

Gary Complete honesty.

Gary closes the sideboard cupboards and then punches the glass one on the upper right side.

He immediately howls with pain as the glass smashes and as he withdraws his right hand we can see it's cut. There's immediately blood running down his forearm, onto his pyjamas and dripping onto the floor.

Maggie *moves quickly for the first aid box in one of the kitchen cupboards,* **Gary** *goes to the sink and runs his hand under the tap before elevating it. It's still bleeding.*

Maggie *approaches him but hesitates before touching him.*

He demurs and **Maggie** *opens the box and immediately sets about patching* **Gary** *up, drying his hand first and examining it.*

Maggie It's not as bad as it looks. But it might need a stitch.

Gary I'm not going up the hospital.

Maggie You might get a nasty scar.

Gary Something to remember tonight by.

Maggie Piss off Gary.

They both hear something upstairs and freeze.

Silence.

Gary That's Annabelle.

They listen for a bit and then **Maggie** *bolts to the kitchen doorway and looks down the hallway towards the bottom of the stairs waiting to see if she comes down.*

Maggie *goes to* **Gary** *and re-takes his injured hand, a little blood seeping through the big plaster covering the cut.*

She binds his hand with some bandage. **Gary** *looks at his iPhone in his free hand, avoiding eye contact.*

Maggie *packs up the first aid box and puts it back in the cupboard it came from. She looks at the mess, she looks at* **Gary**.

Silence.

Maggie Let's just call it a day. I'll go to Mum's.

Gary *looks at her and then back at his iPhone.* **Maggie** *looks at* **Gary** *and all the mess in the kitchen.*

Silence.

Maggie What did you do that for?

Gary What's the point . . .

Maggie What d'you mean what's the point?

Gary You're leaving us . . .

Maggie What?

Gary You're leaving me.

They look at each other for a long time, for as long as you think you can get away with.

Gary I do take an interest in the news. Actually.

Maggie I know you do.

Gary *looks at his iPhone.*

Gary Boris is coming out for Vote Leave. And I do read the odd book. I've read *Steven Gerrard: My Story*. And I'm working myself up to *The Hairy Dieters*.

Maggie I know you do.

Silence.

We need to talk, Gary.

Gary Don't you think it's best in the morning, now? Let's just have a tidy up. And I'll go in the spare room. Or you can. Whatever you want.

Maggie It is the morning.

Silence.

Gary Don't you think one of us should go up and see if Annabelle's alright?

Maggie You go . . .

Gary No . . .

Maggie Go on, you go, I'll clear up.

Gary No, you go . . .

Maggie Go on . . .

Gary It's my mess. I made the mess. I'll clear it up.

Maggie Why don't you make yourself a drink?

Gary Honestly . . .

Maggie Just sit down for five minutes. And when I come back down we can clean up together. And we can talk.

Gary *nods. They both hesitate, somehow not wanting to be apart from each other, even for a moment.*

Silence.

Maggie *goes out again.*

Gary *looks about him at all the mess. He notices that the teapot survived as it was next to the kettle and no longer in the sideboard. Then quite suddenly he begins to cry. It pours out of him, all of the agony of the moment. And then quite as suddenly he stops and pulls himself together. Puts the knife down on the island.*

Gary *goes to a long cupboard and retrieves a dustpan and brush and a hoover. He gets down on his knees with the dustpan and brush, beginning with the remains of the milk jug.*

Maggie *comes in.* **Gary** *looks at her.*

Maggie She's sound asleep.

Gary That's good.

Maggie As I was looking at her . . . I was looking at her . . .

Maggie starts to cry, great hulking sobs. She holds her arms out as if she wants **Gary** *to come and comfort her.*

Gary *hesitates, silence, save for the sound of her crying. Then he goes to her and holds her. They stand there holding each other, just holding each other, for as long as you think you can get away with.*

Maggie's *upset and tears gradually fall away.*

Silence.

Maggie *becomes self-conscious and breaks away from* **Gary**, *wondering what she's doing, and heading for the hoover.*

Gary *watches her as she uncoils the lead, plugs it in and begins to hoover up quite blithely, just ignoring the bits of china that are too big to be sucked up.*

Eventually she stops. **Gary** *is still watching her. She picks up the remainder of the milk jug* **Gary** *had before. Looks at it.*

Gary I wasn't aiming at you.

Maggie I wouldn't blame you if you were.

Gary It was just a . . .

Maggie I honestly wouldn't blame you if you were.

Gary Are you okay?

Maggie Been better.

Silence.

Are you okay?

Gary Been better.

Gary *doesn't know what to say, so he begins to collect up by hand and with the dustpan the bigger bits of crockery.*

Maggie *helps too. It all goes in the bin.*

Silence.

Maggie   I don't know what you must think of me.

Silence.

I mean . . . If it was you got up in the middle of the night and said all this to me . . . I'd have already slung you out.

Silence.

Gary   Do you want to leave?

Maggie   Do you want me to leave?

Gary   No.

Maggie   Even after what I've said?

Gary   No. I love you Maggie. I love you.

Gary *retrieves his iPhone and goes to the bluetooth speaker, which he switches on.*

He quickly finds something on his iPhone and presses play. 'My Lover's Prayer' by Otis Redding plays.

Gary *sways in time to it, looking intently at* **Maggie**.

Maggie   Turn it off, Gary.

Gary   This is our song.

Maggie   Turn it off.

Gary *ignores her and begins to sing all the words.* **Maggie** *folds her arms.*

Gary *begins to sway and dance, doing all he can to attract her attention and make her laugh but she refuses. Avoiding his looks and moving away from him when he gets near her. It becomes a bit outlandish in places.*

Maggie *can stand it no longer and switches off the bluetooth speaker.*

Silence.

Gary   I love you Maggie.

Gary *is genuinely thrown and panicked. He needs a moment to calm himself.*

Silence.

Maggie Are you alright?

Gary I don't know whether I'm coming or going, Mag.

Maggie I will always love you, Gary.

Gary You know, you're fucking with my head.

They look at each other for a long time, for as long as you think you can get away with.

Gary D'you mind if I have an emergency vape?

Maggie *nods and* **Gary** *goes to a drawer and takes out a vape.* **Gary** *catches her eye.*

Gary You don't want me to go outside, do you?

She shakes her head and he begins to vape. Trying to compose himself.

Silence.

Maggie What's that smell?

Gary It's Chewberry Cosmic Fog.

Maggie What?

Gary Strawberry and passion fruit. I like the tropical flavour.

Maggie *watches him vape.*

Silence.

Gary I'm lonely. I'm bored. I feel shit about myself.

Maggie I'm sorry.

Silence.

Gary I can't put it eloquent like you. I thought it was just getting older. You're suddenly self-conscious about the years left on the clock. If you're lucky. I'm not happy either Mag. But I just thought, it's middle age.

Maggie Middle age?

Gary Serious.

Maggie Sixty's middle-aged.

Gary Is it?

Maggie We're young . . .

Gary We're not.

Silence.

I know I'm simple. I like my time with you. My time with Annabelle. Family time. I like my holidays. I like having a beer up town, I like going fishing, I like going over West Ham. I like a round of golf. I like cooking. You have no idea how much pleasure I was gonna get out of that pork belly at lunchtime. Getting the crackling just right. Watching Dad test it. And Mum twinkling. Giving Annabelle the best bit. And you laughing. And sighing. And shaking your head. At the ludicrousness. Of my small pleasures. But now all I've got in my head is John.

Silence.

I didn't want this.

Maggie Neither did I.

Gary You think you're the only one that's had to compromise?

Maggie I'm sure I'm not.

Gary Well you're not, babe.

Maggie I know.

Gary I've put up with things.

Maggie I'm sure you have.

Maggie *puts the knife in the sink and replaces the Febreze in the cupboard. She looks at* **Gary**.

Gary Do you think doing what I do is a piece of piss?

Maggie I know it's not.

Gary The only reason I do what I do is because I can't do nothing else.

Maggie You could do other things.

Gary I couldn't.

Maggie You could if you wanted to.

Gary It's what I'm cut out for. I don't mind saying it. It's the truth. When Joey Jones saw me knocking out man-made leather handbags on Romford Market. And I was just a kid. He said to me when you've done your exams. You're coming up town with me boy. I don't mind it. I'm a City Boy. It's what I am.

Silence.

I was in the Square Mile and I've been on The Wharf for thirty-odd year and I'm tired, Maggie.

Silence.

I say to myself. Another five years and you'll be mortgage free. And Annabelle's school fees and her university money. I'll have it. It will all be set up.

Silence.

But I'm a fraction of the man I was when I went up town. A husk.

Silence.

I used to be the youngest on my desk. Now it's like 'What's that dozy old Tuesday' still doing here.

Silence.

They roll out the putting mat on a Friday afternoon. Right in the middle of the office.

And there's a monkey bet on this. And a double monkey bet on that. And it's 'Come on Gary, liven up. Come on Gary, join in. Come on Gary, put your hand in your pocket'.

Silence.

And I'm there sometimes with that putter in my hand. Looking down the mat, looking at the ball. Everyone gathered round. And I'm shaking like a leaf.

Silence.

But you can't show no weakness. Not even a flicker.

Silence.

You've no idea what it's been like. What it's like. The Stress.

Silence.

I've been living on my nerves.

Silence.

You think I want to be out three nights a week? With those wankers. Frankly.

Silence.

Maggie Then pack it in.

Gary I can't.

Silence.

Maggie You could do something else you enjoyed.

Gary There's plenty of things I'd enjoy . . .

Maggie Then go for it. Now . . .

Gary But there ain't none of them pays like I get paid now, Mag, and you know it . . .

Maggie I didn't want all this . . . It's ridiculous we're spending all that money sending Annabelle to Brentwood Prep . . .

Gary I don't want nothing but the best for her . . .

Silence.

Maggie We don't need a six-bedroom house on the Mount. We never have.

Gary But what about what I want?

Maggie You earn fantastic money. And yet we've got a great big mortgage round our necks. And we're still up against it. And for what? I never wanted this.

Silence.

Gary I always dreamed we'd have three or four kids . . .

Maggie But it's just us, Gary.

Silence.

Gary Well we've got enough room for everyone to come at Christmas.

Maggie We've been in here for seven years and we've never had everyone for Christmas.

Gary Well I can't help it if my lot and your lot don't click.

Maggie Okay, Gary.

Silence.

Gary I don't mean this as an insult. I really don't. But the trouble with you, Maggie, is you've never had to scratch around for a few quid.

Silence.

You try growing up with a dad on the bins and a mum who works in Iceland. You try growing up without a tanner in your pocket. With a house that's always a state. Cos no one ain't got no money to fix nothing. Or do nothing. You try sharing a bedroom with your brother till you're eighteen. You go to a school where no one don't care about learning nothing. They don't care about nothing. Except bunking off and sniffing glue. You try it. Because if you did you might understand why I am the way I am.

Silence.

You was lucky.

Maggie I know.

Gary You had a nice house in Gidea Park.

Maggie It wasn't flash.

Gary You went to a good school.

Maggie And I'm glad I did.

Gary We grew up two mile away from each other. But it might as well have been a different planet.

Maggie Put the violin away, Gary, it doesn't suit you.

Gary Why have your family always looked down on me?

Silence.

Maggie They don't, they love you.

Gary They love me, and they look down on me.

Maggie They don't.

Gary Be honest. They find me crass. They find my taste naff. When I told your mum I was thinking of buying us a villa in Fuengirola, she looked like I'd had a Jimmy Riddle in her Lapsang Souchong.

Silence.

Your dad's the washing machine and appliance man out of Cambridge Heath Road. And your nan had the bakers on

Devon's Road. Since when did your lot get to walk about like their shit don't stink?

Maggie My mum and dad worked hard and did well for themselves.

Gary I know they did.

Silence.

Maggie I'm proud of my dad and the way he built his business. I'm proud of the way my mum worked her way up for the NatWest.

Gary Don't you think I'm proud of my mum and dad?

Maggie Well they've not exactly done very much.

Silence.

Gary They survived.

Silence.

They didn't have a pot to piss in. And they brought up three kids. All doing alright. All of us. They bought our house off the council in nineteen-eighty-three and twenty-five years later they paid off their mortgage. I don't know how they did it.

When you're standing where I'm standing. It's a miracle they managed. Don't look down your nose at my family. Don't you dare.

Maggie I don't. I love them.

Silence.

Gary What have I done so wrong?

Maggie What?

Gary In your mum and dad's eyes.

Maggie You haven't done anything wrong.

Gary When all I've done is provide for you. And Annabelle. And give you everything you want.

Silence.

Maggie They don't like the way you spoil Annabelle.

Silence.

And neither do I.

Gary I don't spoil her.

Maggie You do Gary.

Gary I don't understand why everything has to be so Victorian?

Maggie It doesn't.

Gary She's a kid.

Maggie And she needs boundaries.

Gary She's eight.

Maggie She needs to appreciate the value of things.

Gary She's eight, she's not eighteen.

Maggie I feel like she's growing up easy come easy go . . .

Gary She's not.

Maggie And because I'm the one that always says no. That has always said no. It can be really horrible. It is really horrible for me. You don't support me . . .

Gary When Annabelle's out of order I support you.

Maggie When she bites me.

Silence.

When she kicks me.

Silence.

When she pulls my hair and screams. Then you support me. But what's the point of me ever saying no? When you arrive on the scene and it's, yes Annabelle, whatevs Annabelle.

Silence.

Sometimes she looks at me and I'm convinced she hates me. She looks at me as if I'm shit. Like I am an actual piece of shit.

Gary She doesn't.

Maggie She does.

Gary She doesn't, babe.

Maggie She does.

Gary You're her mum.

Maggie I know she loves me.

Gary She adores you.

Maggie But she hates me. Just as much. Because I say no. I say no on the school run. I say no after Kids Club. I say no after football. I say no before dancing. I say no. Not until you've done your piano practice. I say no at dinner time. Not until you've done your homework. I say no about the telly, about her iPad, about her Xbox, about sleepovers, about what she'll wear and what she won't wear.

Silence.

You have no idea how much I resent you for it Gary. You've reduced my relationship with my daughter to being the person who says no. Because you can't be arsed. You want the easy option.

Silence.

Gary I want her to have nice things. All the things I never had . . .

Maggie You buy her whatever she wants. She doesn't even have to wait for her birthday or Christmas!

Gary You're exaggerating!

Maggie I want you to support me. I want you to say no.

Silence.

I know you've already been talking to her about getting a phone . . .

Gary I swear I haven't . . .

Maggie You have Gary, she's eight . . .

Gary Well I've told her she's not having a phone until she goes to big school. I told her when we was at Bluewater. It ain't happening babe. Move away from the area of Vodafone.

Silence.

I know I can be a better dad. I know I can be a better husband. I know I can.

Maggie It's too late.

Silence.

Gary And what about what I want?

Maggie Like what, Gary?

Gary Like the support I need.

Maggie What support?

Silence.

Gary Well what do you think?

Maggie I'm not a mind-reader, Gary.

Gary In life. You never ask me how I am.

Maggie Yes I do.

Gary You don't, Maggie. You just think, he's alright. It's obvious. Gary, he's alright. He's always alright. Plods along.

Silence.

Maggie I don't.

Gary When was the last time you asked me how I am?

Silence.

Maggie I asked you earlier.

Gary In a normal setting.

Silence.

Maggie I asked you how you were when you came in on Friday...

Gary No you didn't...

Maggie I'm sure I did, I'm sure I said 'How are you? How was your day?'

Gary You didn't, I remember exactly what you said...

Maggie Are you going to quibble over words?

Gary You said 'Do you fancy a Chinese? Because I quite fancy a king prawn with cashew nuts'.

Maggie That's not all I said...

Gary No. And then after half an hour going through the menu. Humming and ah-ing. You decided you wanted an Indian!

Maggie What can I say? I'm a woman, I'm fickle.

Gary And then when it come. You didn't eat hardly anything. And you didn't say much either.

Maggie Well now you know why.

Silence.

Gary You never ask me about work. You avoid talking about my family.

Maggie I don't.

Gary You do. You do, Mag. We both know.

Silence.

You take no interest in me. You just think 'Gary, he's alright'.

Maggie Well you hardly take an interest in me.

Silence.

Gary I've wanted us to be close.

Maggie So have I.

Gary I've missed you so much.

Silence.

Maggie I don't know what good this is doing.

Gary I don't understand why you just let things dwindle . . .

Maggie What?

Gary In our sex life.

Silence.

Gary I know a woman has her time. In the month. That's just life. But apart from that time. You know. We was always a once in the week, once at the weekend couple.

Maggie To begin with. Literally years ago. We had Annabelle. You're always out Gary.

Gary I'm not out five nights a week. I'm not out all weekend.

Silence.

I know all those years. Trying for Annabelle. Fucking hell, sex when you're trying for a baby. As a bloke you spend years of your life dreaming of being with a woman. Who wants you to give her one every day of the week. And not only that. Puts it in your diary so you can look forward to it!

Silence.

I tell you what. If I had to have double pie, double mash and liquor six days in a row, I'd go off of it. And double pie, double mash and liquor is my death row meal.

Maggie Double pie, double mash and liquor?

Gary Yes, babe.

Maggie It's not necessarily an analogy that would've sprung to my mind.

Silence.

Gary We all know what it's like when you've got a baby. There's a sexual desert and we're all travelling through it. In search of water. Sexy water. But there's nothing as far as the eye can see. Just the odd dune. Maybe a nomad. You're on your camel. I'm on my camel. And then! An oasis! It's Wednesday morning and you're both awake before the alarm's gone off! And the baby's still asleep. And I look at you and you look at me. And my hand goes up your back. And you hook your leg over And hell's bells, Annabelle's awake and she's screaming the house down. We all know.

Maggie *laughs, really laughs.* **Gary** *smiles. They become self-conscious.*

Silence.

Gary You're right. Annabelle never gets up in the night. I wanted more.

Maggie What d'you mean?

Gary I wanted more.

Maggie More sex?

Silence.

Gary You just want it over with. I'm just trying to do what you want.

Silence.

We did used to have sexy sex. Didn't we?

Maggie I thought we did.

Gary I haven't stopped being a man. I needed you. I wanted us to try things. To get things going. I wanted us to be connected.

Maggie Try things?

Gary Yeah?

Maggie What sort of things? Not kinky things?

Silence.

Gary You know . . . Whatever you fancy. 'Hello Mrs Maggie, I'm your friendly gas fitter here to clean your pipes. Oh dear! What's that inside my tool bag? I must have put a nine-inch dildo in there by mistake. What a palaver!'

Maggie Do you honestly think that's what I want?

Gary I don't know what you want. Can't you see I'm clutching at straws here, babe?

Silence.

Maggie I've just gone off it.

Gary What?

Maggie You know what.

Silence.

Gary But don't you want to try?

Maggie I tried last weekend. And it made me feel like shit.

Silence.

Gary I know you think no one looks twice at him. But you're not the only one who can still turn a head on occasion.

Silence.

Maggie You're not having an affair are you, Gary?

Maggie *is horrified and involuntarily puts her hands across her chest as if to protect her heart.*

Silence.

Gary No I'm not. But if Veronica in Finance had her way I'd be doing more than taking down my receipts once a week.

Maggie Who the hell is this Veronica?

Maggie *wants to cry but won't.*

Silence.

Gary *and* **Maggie** *look at each other.*

Silence.

Maggie Is this it? Is this what we've become?

Gary Maggie, listen to me.

Maggie Maggie? Now I know I'm in trouble . . .

Silence.

Gary Mag, listen to me.

Maggie I'm sorry I'm just upset . . .

Maggie *really wants to cry hard again but resists it with all her might.*

Gary *goes to her, wanting to comfort her.*

Maggie No Gary.

Gary I need a hug. I need comfort. Don't you think I need that?

Silence.

You're leaving me.

Maggie If I was leaving you I would have said.

Silence.

I did talk to John about leaving you.

Gary Did you?

Maggie I did.

Silence.

Gary What did he say?

Maggie He said it's too soon.

Gary Did he?

Maggie Yeah.

Gary I must say, I am surprised.

Silence.

Maggie He said 'we've both got family responsibilities'.

Gary Right.

Maggie He said the romance died with her a long time ago. But there's still loyalty.

Gary Loyalty?

Maggie And family love.

Gary Family love?

Maggie He said he can't let the carnal feelings . . . He said.

Silence.

He said there's no way he can get into us leaving our partners at the minute. He's very caring is John and his wife's not well.

Gary Right.

Maggie He's that sort of man. Upright.

Gary Yeah. He sounds like a lovely fella.

Silence.

What are you going to do then, Mag?

Silence.

Maggie I thought I could go in one of the guest rooms.

Gary Right.

Maggie For a while.

Gary Right.

Maggie Until we've worked out what we're going to do.

Gary So what is it exactly you're trying to work out, babe?

Silence.

Maggie I thought we could have a period of reflection.

Gary A period of reflection?

Maggie I read an article on the internet.

Gary Right.

Maggie A period of calm reflection.

Gary Calm reflection?

Maggie Yeah.

Gary So what? Are we still having dinner together? And doing things with Annabelle together?

Maggie Yes.

Gary But you're in your own room?

Maggie Or if you want to. You can go in one of the spare rooms . . .

Gary D'you want me to go in one of the spare rooms?

Maggie Only if you want to.

Gary I don't know.

Maggie I mean it would make more sense.

Gary What would?

Maggie Most of the clothes and shoes and everything in our room is my stuff.

Gary What are we going to tell Annabelle?

Maggie I don't know.

Maggie *gets upset, holds it in.*

Silence.

Maggie Can we still be friends?

Gary I don't think they do conscious uncoupling in Essex. Unconscious coupling, yep. But not the other way round.

Maggie *laughs, wants to cry, doesn't.*

Silence.

Gary And where does John sit in this? In this period of calm reflection. I'll tell you what for nothing. Not in the fucking garage manhandling my golf clubs.

Silence.

Maggie I want to keep in touch with him.

Gary Right.

Maggie I want to see him.

Gary Right.

Maggie I won't go to bed with him. I promise you.

Silence.

If this is the end. If this is the beginning of the end. Then I want us to do it as well as we can. For us. For Annabelle. For our families. One day we will all be friends.

Gary *gets upset, holds it in.*

Silence.

Gary *looks at her.*

Silence.

Gary What do you want Maggie?

Maggie I don't even know any more . . .

Gary What do you want? What did you want?

Maggie What?

Gary I want to understand you. Please. Let me.

Maggie *nods, thinks.*

Silence.

Maggie I think . . . Until I was eighteen. This might seem. Ridiculous. My life was absolutely brilliant. Like there were little disappointments. But life was so content. It was so happy. With Mum and Dad and my brothers. I loved school. I loved Coopers. All my mates and my teachers. I wasn't very good at sport. I wasn't someone who had lots of boyfriends. I wasn't that bothered. I loved my mates. And I knew blokes fancied me. So it was alright. I didn't care. It didn't matter.

Silence.

In the sixth form I really wanted a VW Beetle. And the summer before uni I learned to drive. I thought I've got to pass my test before I go to Exeter. I have to. I did. And I noticed about a week after I got my A-Level results. About a fortnight before my nineteenth birthday. I noticed this grey VW Beetle. A bit bashed up. But it was parked around the corner from Mum and Dad's. On the corner of Heaton

Grange Road. And I thought Mum and Dad have got me it for my birthday. For when I go to uni.

Silence.

And every day I walked past it. Like I had a summer job in Boots in Romford. And every day I went out of my way to go past it. On my way to work. To check it was still there.

And I day-dreamed.

Silence.

I counted down the days until my birthday. I imagined driving it down the M4 to uni. Full of all my stuff. I was thinking about seeing it out of the window of my room in halls. I never parked it under a tree. I was already planning my days down at the beach at Exmouth.

Silence.

All of this going on in my mind. I was also like. I have to name her.

Gary Who?

Maggie My car.

Gary Oh.

Maggie I decided I was going to call her Beryl.

Gary Why?

Maggie She looked like a Beryl. Anyway, you know, I was off. You have no idea what my imagination could be like. I've never wanted anything more in my entire life than that car. Neither before nor since. It sounds ridiculous but it's true.

Silence.

Anyway, the day of my birthday came. And I looked at the presents from my brothers. And Mum and Dad. And I saw it. I couldn't take my eyes off it. There was a little square box.

That Mum and Dad said I should save until last. It was the keys. It was the keys to Beryl.

Silence.

And I opened the little box last. And there was a beautiful ring. You remember it? It was a ruby, with diamonds. And mum had tears in her eyes. 'We knew how much you loved your Grandma's ring. Your Grandma wouldn't have wanted anyone but you to have it.' And I said 'but Beryl'. And I was up and out and out of the front door. Round the corner into Heaton Grange Road. And Beryl was gone. The car was gone. I walked across the road into Raphael's Park. And I raged and howled. I turned myself inside out. No one could fathom it.

Silence.

It was such a knock. Nothing had ever gone wrong before.

Silence.

Dad had sorted me out a car as it goes. Before I went to Exeter. An old Fiesta. Uni was alright. The English degree was alright. I met some alright people. There was a lot of drinking and shagging. And posh boys. Rugby boys. Some of the girls I lived with were gross. Worse than the boys. Nothing about it was bohemian. I should have just left really. But you don't just pack in when you come from a family like mine.

Silence.

I wrote hundreds of letters. To TV companies, film companies, magazines, newspapers, everywhere. Nothing. A mate of a mate of a mate worked with Terry Christian. And arranged a coffee. But he cancelled. I graduated, I was back home. Me and Mum weren't getting on. Uncle William knew someone who had a Junior HR position in an insurance firm up town. And there you go. Bosh. Thirty years later. I've counted my blessings for thirty years, Gary. And I feel very lucky to earn a good wage, To have a good job. But I wanted to do something I enjoyed.

Silence.

I did make one friend at uni I kept for a bit. She was doing English with me. Jo. Joanna. She wanted to work in TV like me. She really struggled as well. Did all sorts of jobs.

Temping and waitressing. She was in a shared house down in Turnpike Lane. She kept saying to me. Come and live with me. And I was all geared up to. And then she got this job as a runner for Carlton Television. Remember them? And I couldn't handle it. I was so angry. I was jealous and silly. And I let the friendship go. I let Jo go. But I couldn't let the feeling go. I've never been able to let the feeling go.

Silence.

This isn't what I wanted.

Silence.

We're friends on Facebook. We connected when I had Annabelle. She saw a picture another uni random commented on and . . . And we started to be in touch a bit.

Gary I remember you going to see her.

Maggie Yeah.

Gary You said you had a top afternoon.

Maggie Hmm.

Silence.

There's no direct way to get to Crouch End. It's really annoying. I got the train to Liverpool Street. And walked round to Moorgate. Annabelle was a nightmare. Got the train back out to Hornsey. I was an hour early. I was so paranoid about getting there. And I thought I can't knock on the door an hour early. So I had a wander round Crouch End.

Silence.

Annabelle perked up. I went in Gail's for a coffee. Had a cinnamon bun. And I started to dream.

Silence.

I was the TV producer. Not Jo.

Silence.

I was looking in the window of this boutique. A street fashion boutique you could say. I caught my reflection in the window. Annabelle holding my hand. And she said to me 'Mummy why are you crying?'

Silence.

And I thought pull yourself together, Maggie. You don't want Jo to see you like this. And the more I told myself to pull myself together. That made it even worse. By time I got to the top of Jo's road I could hardly put one foot in front of the other. And it had started to rain. And Annabelle was getting in on the act. Grizzling and sniffing and sobbing. And I thought my heartache isn't even my own any more.

Silence.

Maggie   So we just came home.

Silence.

That was when I started to force the issue of going back to work.

Silence.

Why do people ever see things through? Why do they ever stay? It's so hard.

Silence.

I want a new life, Gary.

Silence.

Gary I had no idea, babe, I . . .

Silence.

Why've you never talked to me like this before?

Maggie I didn't think I could.

Gary Why are you saying that?

Maggie You never seemed interested in me. You only ever seemed interested in Annabelle.

Gary You can talk to me . . .

Maggie I can't, Gary. It's always just banter with you.

Silence.

Gary Everyone's disappointed. Everyone's got regrets. Everyone wonders. That's just what it is to be human. To be a person. And to be alive. Life's hard. Life is hard. And the older you get the harder it gets.

Silence.

To me it's about the little things. They get you through.

He glances at the pork belly on the plate.

Having Mum and Dad round for a roast to say thank you. Everyone having a laugh. Scrutinising the crackling. Not too pliable. Not too much un-rendered fat. But you don't want to chip your tooth on it.

Silence.

Maggie What did you want Gary? What do you want? Go on. Tell me. Don't be scared. Say whatever you want.

Silence.

Gary I've got everything I ever wanted.

Maggie You've got everything you ever wanted?

Gary Yeah.

Maggie *is flabbergasted.*

Maggie But what are you going to do with the rest of your life, Gary?

Silence.

Surely there must be things, there must have been things . . .

Gary I would have liked a bigger family. But you know that.

Silence.

You talk like most of our marriage. Twelve, thirteen years of a marriage. Don't count for nothing. Except heartache and pain. Fine you feel what you feel. You've said what you've said. But don't mug me off with this bullshit that our whole marriage is shit just because you've had your head turned.

Silence.

I've heard what you've said, Mag. Every single word. You know what? You let me take Annabelle in hand from now on. Let me do it. And we're getting a babysitter in once a week now. So we can go out. And if your lot are offended. Or my lot are offended. I'll straighten them out. And I get what you're saying about . . . I get it. I get it.

Silence.

I promise you I won't ask you for no sex. I promise you. I swear. We've got to get things straight . . . You want calm reflection. I will give you calm reflection. If you want me to go in one of the spare rooms I will. I don't mind the one at the back. I'll go in that one. I get it, Mag . . .

Maggie Gary . . .

Gary And you know what? I know I've got to pack in up town. I know I have. It's killing me. You're right. Next thing, you know, I'll drop down dead. There's something else I can do there's bound to be . . . I can re-train. There's something. I'll find something, Mag. You see.

Silence.

And if you want to downsize and move somewhere else. Then we can talk about it. We can. I'm open to ideas, Mag, I am. I promise you I am. If that's what you want. That's what we're doing. If you want move to Crouch End, we can move to Crouch End.

Maggie Changing everything isn't going to change everything anymore. Not inside. Not inside . . .

Gary I know, I know . . .

Maggie I'm tired of hoping and dreaming. And waiting and wishing. And telling myself it will all be alright in the end. I'm tired Gary. I'm tired.

They look at each other for a long time, for as long as you think you can get away with.

Gary Look . . . I'll take Annabelle football. We can put on a nice show for Mum and Dad. They won't stay long. And when Annabelle's gone to bed tonight we can talk. Sensible like.

Maggie Can we?

Gary *finds courage.*

Silence.

Gary I've got to be honest about one thing. I've got to be honest about myself. About the sort of fella I am.

Silence.

You saying about keeping seeing John? It's asking too much of me.

Silence.

Fine, you want to try and work out what you want to do. I'm gutted. I'm more devastated by this than you'll ever know, darling. But I'm a big boy. I'll deal with it. And I'll fight for you. I'll fight for my marriage. I'll fight like you've never seen me fight in all my life. But I'm flesh and blood. I'm flesh and blood.

Silence.

If you're going on seeing John then our marriage is as good as over.

Silence.

But Mag, babe . . . You know what I think? This isn't the end. This isn't the end for us. No way. We've not even got anywhere near the end of the road. This is the middle. This is the middle. This is *The Empire Strikes Back*.

Maggie You want me to give up John?

Gary *nods.* **Maggie** *thinks, gets upset, holds it in.*

Silence.

Gary At least give us half a chance, darling.

They look at each other for a long time, for as long as you think you can get away with.

Maggie We're miles apart, Gary, literally miles apart.

Gary Okay, okay.

Maggie I don't know how we can possibly come together?

Silence.

Gary I can't be a completely different person, Mag. I'm nearly fifty years of age. I am what I am. I mean all the things I said. It's not Gary-bants this time, babe. I will do things better.

Gary *finds courage.*

I can't completely change your life. Only you can do that. And if that's what you really want then let's call it a day.

Gary *takes in their big kitchen.*

I don't care about any of this really. You're all I ever wanted. It's a rut. We're in a massive rut. We'll get through it.

Maggie Will we, though?

Gary *hesitates, silence.*

Gary I think I'm a bit low. I think I've been like it for a long time. For years.

Silence.

It's weird, I thought not wanting anything anymore was a sign of contentment. But it's not, is it? It's the opposite. I'm not putting it on you. I know it's down to me. But it takes a lot of bollocks for me to admit it. You know?

Maggie Thank you. Thank you.

Silence.

Gary I feel really old. All of a sudden I feel really old.

Maggie So do I.

She looks at him, uncertain.

Gary All I want is little bit more time. So I can really show you what I'm made of.

Silence.

I'm sure if this John's a decent fella he'll understand. I'm sure if this John really thinks something of you he'll wait for you.

They look at each other for a long time, for as long as you think you can get away with.

Finally **Maggie** *nods.* **Gary** *nods. He goes to the bluetooth speaker and puts on the radio. He turns the volume down. Music from Heart Radio subtly fills the kitchen.*

Maggie *goes to the cupboard and gets out some muesli.*

She goes to the fridge and gets out some milk. She puts them on the island and goes in search of some bowls and spoons. But she remembers **Gary** *smashed all the bowls.*

Maggie *has an idea and ferrets around in another cupboard. She brings out two of Annabelle's Disney bowls from when she was small.* **Gary** *smiles at the sight of the bowls.*

Gary *looks at the broken glass pane in the sideboard and thinks. He has an idea. He goes to the cupboard* **Maggie** *fished out the muesli from and takes out a big box of Frosties. He takes the cereal from the cardboard box and flattens out the cardboard.*

He takes it to the sideboard and holds it up against the frame of the smashed pane in the sideboard. He then gets some scissors from one drawer and some Sellotape from another drawer and cuts the cardboard into a rectangle which will cover over the broken glass pane.

He does it with care, **Maggie** *watches him as he Sellotapes the cardboard into place. He admires his work and looks at* **Maggie**. *They look at each other for a long time, for as long as you think you can get away with.*

Gary *moves and flicks on the kettle and watches it start to re-boil. He takes the teapot and fishes out the tea bags from earlier and chucks them in the bin. And then goes to the sink and gives it a rinse. He can hear something upstairs.*

Gary That's Annabelle.

Maggie *turns off the radio and they both listen.*

Gary She's up.

Maggie *and* **Gary** *look at each other for as long as you think you can get away with.*

Maggie *goes to* **Gary** *they look at each other.* **Gary** *smiles and pats* **Maggie** *on the arm.* **Maggie** *nods, less certain.*

Gary *goes out through the kitchen doorway.*

The kettle boils. **Maggie** *puts two teabags in the teapot and fills it with hot water. She carries the teapot over to the kitchen island. She looks at the empty sideboard and back at the teapot. It survived.*

Fade.

The End.

End

For Mum & For Robert

End was first produced in the Dorfman Theatre at the National Theatre, London, on 20 November 2025, with the following cast and creative team:

Alfie	**Clive Owen**
Julie	**Saskia Reeves**
Director	Rachel O'Riordan
Set and Costume Designer	Gary McCann
Lighting Designer	Sally Ferguson
Sound Designer	Donato Wharton
Intimacy Director	Bethan Clark
Casting	Alastair Coomer CDG
Voice Coach	Cathleen McCarron
Dialect Coach	Patricia Logue
Associate Sound Designer	Nick Mann
Staff Director	Philip J Morris

Mid-June, 2016

The lounge diner of a large terraced house in Harringay, London.

At the lounge end is a sofa. There's a blanket and a pillow on the sofa. At the other end is a dining table.

A window is open and the sound of a little birdsong finds its way into the room. There's a large serving hatch and you can see into the kitchen. The clock on the kitchen wall says ten to seven in the morning.

There are lots of books and the room has a great but discreet audio sound system.

There's an open door leading out towards the hallway, leading to the kitchen and the stairs. Not that we see the whole house but it's big. There are four bedrooms, the loft has been converted and there's a studio at the end of the garden.

Alfie, *58, is standing with the aid of a medical walking stick. He's in an expensive hoodie, a bit too young for him, 2013/14 West Ham home shorts and some Adidas sliders. His medication has taken the edge off his pain.*

His wife, **Julie**, *58, looks at him. She's in a pretty summer dress with pockets, a bit too young for her, too. She has some clothes for* **Alfie** *over her right arm.*

Alfie *finally turns and looks at* **Julie**.

They look at each other for as long as you think you can get away with.

Alfie   I love you darling.

Julie   I love you too.

Alfie   I've accepted what Dr Chan said on Friday.

Julie   Okay.

Alfie   And I've decided I don't want any more treatment.

Julie   What?

Silence.

Alfie I know Mr Rahman thinks I've made the right decision.

Silence.

Julie Have you taken your tablets?

Alfie *nods.* **Julie** *puts down* **Alfie**'s *clothes on the sofa and goes to him.*

They hold each other for a long time, just hold each other. They look at each other, kiss, look at each other again.

Alfie I'll be okay. Are you?

Julie I'm okay.

Alfie What time's Annabelle coming?

Julie About half past eight. Nine.

Alfie Will you help me talk to her?

Silence.

Is Toby coming?

Julie No he's on that stag do. I did say.

Alfie Yeah. Sorry.

Julie He's coming back this afternoon.

Alfie My memory sometimes.

Julie *heads towards the kitchen, stops, turns.*

Julie You don't think Toby would do anything . . .

Alfie What?

Julie You know . . . With his mates. In Amsterdam.

Alfie What?

Julie Annabelle's convinced herself he's up to all sorts with his mates.

Alfie Like what?

Julie You know . . . With a window girl . . .

Alfie How do you know what they're called?

Julie Everyone knows what they're called.

Alfie I'm pulling your leg! Toby probably had a few pints. Went in a coffee shop for a smoke with his mates. Went back to the hotel early and spent the rest of the night with his head down a toilet. That kid can't take his drink. Oh, Ju, I'd give my fucking right bollock. For two days on the turps in Amsterdam . . .

Julie I know, Espresso martini, cheeky little livener and a big fat doobie.

Alfie I'd give both my bollocks. Shrooms. Bosh. A pill. A club. Hair of the dog. Bosh.

Julie *laughs. Silence.*

Julie I think Annabelle said all the lads are in apartments. I bet they're having a right old laugh . . .

Alfie Does it matter?

Julie What?

Alfie Does it matter whether they're in a hotel or apartments?

Julie I was only saying. Chill your boots. Annabelle doesn't like the idea of him being on the stag do with his mates.

Alfie Why?

Julie You know what she's like, she's so serious about everything, Alf . . . I don't know what planet she's on, he's nearly as square as she is . . .

Alfie How on earth did we manage to give birth to Annabelle?

Julie Ahem, I think you'll find it was me that gave birth to her, Alf . . .

Alfie Are you sure there wasn't a moment of passion with Boring Tone when I wasn't looking?

Julie Oh God I've not thought about him in years, what a nerk . . .

Alfie Boring Tone was so boring after speaking to him I needed a lie down for three days . . .

Julie Boring Tone was so boring he used to make me paranoid it was contagious . . .

Alfie *laughs, thinks.*

Alfie Love her dearly though I do, I cannot fathom how us two managed to bring into being Saffy two-point-zero. Go on, break my heart . . .

Julie I've never done anything like that. Have I? Dickhead.

Alfie *laughs. Silence.*

Julie I think with Toby she can see herself settling down properly.

Alfie Can she?

Julie Alf! Have you been living under a rock?

Alfie As far as I'm concerned it's off and then it's on. It's off and then it's on . . .

Julie She trusts him. But she's realising how much she likes him. She feels insecure at the same time.

Alfie The absolute worst Toby will have done is have a little smoke and have a little puke and maybe been to see a sex show . . .

Julie Imagine Annabelle's face?

Alfie I know.

Julie She doesn't honestly think Toby and his mates have gone to Amsterdam to pick her some tulips and look at a painting of a Milkmaid?

Alfie *laughs. Silence.*

Julie I think she had a right old set to with Toby on Friday morning before he went. Don't get annoyed, I've not said . . . But she's been seeing her counsellor again, Alf. Her anxiety's going through the roof.

Alfie You should have told me that . . .

Julie Didn't you try and protect your dad from things? When he was ill.

Silence.

She wants us all to be together this morning. She wants some mummy and daddy love and a bacon sandwich.

Silence.

I don't know how you're going to explain all this to Annabelle. She'll want you to chuck the kitchen sink at it.

Alfie For another year? At best.

Silence.

And what about you, babe?

Julie What about me?

Alfie How are you?

Julie Don't worry about me, Alf.

Silence.

Alfie Do you wish we'd got married?

Julie No. I'm happy as I am.

Alfie Really?

Julie I mean, I'm not happy you're not well . . .

Alfie It's okay.

Julie We've had a wonderful life. I've been so happy.

Alfie Have we?

Julie I think so. Don't you?

Alfie There's other things I want, Ju.

Julie Like what?

Alfie You heard what Dr Chan said. You didn't let go of my hand once. If I stop. Three months. We've got to get things straight. We've got be on the same page here, babe, haven't we?

Julie Right, tea.

Alfie Annabelle's got nothing to worry about with Toby. He's a good kid.

Julie When did you go and see a sex show?

Alfie It was donkeys' years ago. It was on the wind-down after 'Dance Valley'.

Julie Right.

Alfie It was nothing, Ju. What's up? You're never weird about this stuff . . .

Julie I was only asking a question.

Alfie Do you think we'll ever have sex again?

Julie I beg your pardon?

Alfie Do you think we'll ever make love again?

Julie What's all this about now?

Alfie I love you darling.

Julie Of course we will.

Alfie I wonder if we will though?

Silence.

Julie Were you alright coming down?

Alfie I was fine.

Julie I had my heart in my mouth.

Alfie I came down on my bum.

Julie Have you been listening to music?

Alfie Yeah I.

Julie Okay.

Alfie Yeah I want to choose the record.

Julie What for?

Alfie Maybe a couple of records.

Julie Right?

Alfie You know what for.

Julie I don't, Alf.

Alfie For the service.

Julie What, at half past six in the morning?

Alfie Darling, I've spent my whole adult life playing records at half past six in the morning.

Julie *laughs, so does* **Alfie**. *Silence.*

Julie Do you want some tea?

Alfie No.

Julie Shall I make a pot of coffee?

Alfie No, I don't fancy it.

Julie Did you pick one?

Alfie I kind of went down a rabbit hole. I mean obviously. My heart was exploding.

Alfie *fishes his iPhone out of his hoodie pocket, selects the Apple Music app, finds the song and presses play. 'Going Back to My Roots' by Richie Havens plays.*

Alfie I think this tune's a contender.

Alfie *watches* **Julie** *intently, she takes a breath to steady herself, listens. Almost immediately he switches it off.*

Julie   It's okay.

Alfie   It's alright. Annabelle's coming.

Julie   No go on, I want you to.

Alfie   Look, we can do it another time . . .

Julie   So what are you thinking?

Alfie   Erm.

Julie   When do you want them played? Go on. It's okay.

Alfie   I haven't had a chance to think it through properly.

Julie   Okay.

Alfie   We haven't talked about it, have we, Ju? We got to, Ju.

Julie   Well let's talk.

Alfie   You and Annabelle. Music-a. It's been my life.

Julie   I know, love.

Julie *moves to go to him but hesitates, catching the look on his face.*

Alfie   It's alright.

Julie   Let me.

Alfie   If we . . . I won't. I can't.

Julie   Go on, love.

Alfie   I want a good end.

They look at each other for as long as you think you can get away with.

They both use all their willpower and courage to stay present in the room.

Alfie *looks at his iPhone and back at* **Julie**.

Julie It's okay. It's not okay. But it's okay.

Alfie I want a record to play as they carry me out at the end of the service. One of my favourites, Ju. I don't want any of that John Lennon 'Imagine' bollocks.

*****Alfie*** *finds another song and presses play.*

'Total Confusion' by A Homeboy, A Hippie & A Funki Dredd & The Future Sound of London plays.

They listen to a bit. **Alfie** *nods his head.* **Julie** *is horrified.* **Alfie** *switches it off and beams at her.*

Julie You want that?

Alfie Babe, joke. Joke, babe.

*****Alfie*** *laughs his head off and so does* **Julie** *a bit, with relief.*

Julie Prick.

Alfie Always, babe, always been a dickhead.

Julie Fucking prick, honestly.

Alfie Alright, don't rub it in.

They laugh.

Alfie I want to give people a lift at the end. You've got to finish your set with a banger.

*****Alfie*** *finds another song and presses play on his iPhone.*

'Lady (Hear Me Tonight)' by Modjo plays. They listen to a bit, look at each other.

Julie I like this one.

They both nod their heads and **Julie** *dicks about a bit.* **Alfie** *switches it off. Silence.*

Alfie I feel so young.

Julie I know. I always want to dance when I hear this one. I always used to like coming down when it was you and Julius and Tall Paul.

Alfie It was nice. Romain Tranchart put the Acetate in my hand. And I thought fuck it. I put it on the slip mat. And had a little listen. And there's that Chic Nile Rogers guitar. And I'm like let's do it. Let's do it. Let's do it. Ministry exploded. It went off.

Julie I bet.

Alfie It's hard ain't it?

Julie Yeah. Really hard.

Alfie I'm thinking about Mum. Singing in the kitchen. Peeling the potatoes. And Nan. Mum and Nan thick as thieves. In the Pie and Mash. Mum eating jellied eels and Nan eating stewed eels. Mug of tea and false teeth on the table. And Mum and Dad dancing in the sitting room on a Sunday. Mum playing her seven-inch singles. Motown and Atlantic. Me and Dad dicking around singing 'I'm Forever Blowing Bubbles'. Shall we park all this until later?

Julie I'm alright, Alf.

Alfie You sure, Ju?

Julie What's on your mind?

Alfie He's nice that Dr Chan.

Julie It's hard to accept, Alfie.

Alfie Got a nice way about him.

Julie Would you accept it? If it was me?

Alfie I'm sure I wouldn't. If the boot was on the other foot I daresay I'd want you to chuck the kitchen sink at it.

Julie Well then. We've got be on the same page on this one haven't we, babe?

Alfie We have.

Julie Go on, spit it out.

Alfie I want to go home. I want to be with Mum and Dad. And Nan. Up at London Road cemetery. I know we've lived here a long time now, babe. I know I've done a thing or two in my life but I don't want to be in Highgate Cemetery. With Karl Marx and Malcolm-fucking-McLaren.

Silence.

I'm from Collier Row. I'm an Essex Boy. I don't know no one there.

Julie Okay we can go there. When the time comes we can be laid to rest together there.

Alfie I want to be in with my mum and my dad. And my nan. I don't want to be on my own.

Julie But I thought we'd be together?

Julie *wants to cry, doesn't.*

Alfie What?

Julie I thought, not for a long, long time. But. Like. I've had this notion. It's got me by.

Julie *exercises all her willpower so she doesn't cry.*

Alfie When the time comes you can be with me up at Brentwood . . .

Julie What your mum and your dad and your nan – and me and you – all in together?

Alfie Yeah.

Julie You can only put four in one plot. Your mum didn't like me, Alf.

Alfie Don't be like that.

Julie It's alright. You've told me now. I'm fine with it. It doesn't matter.

Alfie Go on. I'm all ears.

Julie I've been trying to block a lot out. But when I have. You know?

Alfie Yeah.

Julie I've been telling myself this story. Walking over, over Harringay Station, through Crouch End. And over Suicide Bridge. Stopping for some flowers on Highgate Hill. Ambling through Waterlow Park. I've always loved Waterlow Park. Looking at the city. The Shard on the tree line. Then coming to see you. A headstone of a carved book. You on the left page and some space for me on the right. And the words. Our words. 'I have loved thee with an everlasting love.'

Alfie That's all gone through your mind? Is there any chance I could have some engravings as well?

Julie Engravings? Like what?

Alfie A Twelve Hundred. And a glitterball. And a smoke machine. With a little strawberry tab. So everyone knows it's the same flavour as the one Danny had at Shoom.

Julie Right?

Alfie And maybe perched on the arm of the turntable. A Hammerette in a low-cut top. Showing a bit of tit. Look class that on a gravestone.

Alfie *pulls a face.*

Julie You are such a dickhead. You're such a fucking cock.

Alfie *laughs, so does* **Julie**.

Alfie 'I have loved thee with an everlasting love.' Is that it? Is that the words?

Julie Yeah.

Alfie That's so beautiful. You should be a writer.

Julie Fuck off.

Alfie I'm proud of you. You know I am.

Julie Shall we have some tea? Alf?

Alfie I am. I was so proud of you when your book came out. I've been proud of all of them. Every single one.

Julie Alfie it's such a pain to get from Harringay to the cemetery in Brentwood.

Alfie Ju . . .

Julie When I want to come and see you I've either got to drive. Or I've got to get the chugga-chugga to Wanstead Park, walk down to Forest Gate and come back out again . . . For Christ's sake, Alf. It's not going to be you is it, on your birthday? Or Christmas? I've never begrudged you anything have I, babe?

Alfie No, I'll be having a nice long kip in the ground. It's what I want, Ju.

Julie Honestly, I'll have you excavated and moved in the middle of the night!

Alfie No! You can't do that!

They both laugh.

Julie Well you've got it off your chest now. I'm glad you've said what you wanted to say.

Alfie I haven't.

Julie What?

Alfie I haven't said what I wanted to say.

Julie What there's more?

They look at each other for as long as you think you can get away with.

Alfie The thing I find really overwhelming. The thing I find really hard.

Julie Go on.

Alfie I'm not actually scared of going. I know I'll just go to sleep in the end. That's all it is. I just won't wake up.

Silence.

Julie Go on, you can do it. You can say it.

Alfie It's the before.

Julie What do you mean?

Alfie You know what it was like with Dad. About a week before he went. And he had all of his marbles. And we talked. Every time I said goodbye. I said 'Bye, Dad. See you tomorrow. I love you, Dad'. And we never ever said I love you, did we?

Julie No.

Alfie And he'd make a joke of it. 'I love you boy. Go on fuck off home. I'll see you tomorrow.'

Julie *laughs.*

Alfie I always turned round to look at him one last time before I went out of his room. And I could see in his eyes. And he could see in my eyes. In my whole demeanour. It's like. How many more times are we going look each other? Is this it?

Silence.

You know? How many more times will I come round the North Circular and drop off on to the Chigwell Road. Up through Collier Row. And all those thoughts of being boy. Of the view from Lawns Park. The city. London. Where I knew I always wanted to be. Just before I went down the hill on my sledge. You know? Make a right into Broxhill Road and then a sharp left into St Francis's. Again. Is he here? Is he still with us? He's still here. Running out of puff. I go in to his room. I kiss him. Smell him. Dad. The smell of his hair. Dad. We look at each other. The relief. In both of us. Last time wasn't the last time.

Silence.

That feeling. Strangely euphoric. It's gone right away. Fuck. This is it. This is the last time. The hurt. I don't want that.

Alfie *gathers himself, closes his eyes, uses all his strength to stay composed.*

Julie　What do you mean, darling?

Alfie　When I was boy playing in the garden. I saw a snake. It was a summer's morning. Like this morning. And I was in the garden. I was terrified. I properly shit myself. I would have been eight. That's it. It was. The summer West Ham won the World Cup . . .

Julie　Honestly . . .

Alfie　What?

Julie　How many times have I heard that shit joke?

Alfie *laughs.* **Julie** *laughs.*

Alfie　It must have been the first time in my life. I'd had the conscious thought 'I'm going to die'. Then Dad put his hand on my shoulder. And he said 'It's only an old English grass snake, boy. He won't bite. He's not interested in you. Now, an adder. He's a different kettle of fish. He might bite. But you'll know how to spot him. Because he's got a zig-zag pattern down his back. And he's got red eyes.' I said, 'red eyes?' He said 'Yes son, red eyes, like the devil'. I said 'I don't want to play in the garden anymore'. And when I was that age I spent all summer in the garden. And you know what Dad said? He said, 'Son, I tell you what I'm going to do. I'm going to go in my toolbox and get you my hammer. The big one. And you if you see an adder. You give him a great big fucking whack on the head'.

Alfie *laughs.* **Julie** *laughs.*

Alfie When I was a kid the six weeks summer holiday felt like it was endless. And then it was August bank holiday. Mum and Dad screaming and shouting about the cost of my new school uniform. And then one day it starts to rain.

Julie How come you've never told me that story?

Alfie I didn't want you to put it in a book.

Julie What?

Silence.

Alfie I've not thought about it in years. I've been thinking about all sorts of things this morning. Romford's become part of London. But when we was kids, it was separate. It was Essex. Wasn't it, darling?

Julie What are you saying all this for, Alf?

Alfie Once I'm ready to be moved in to St John's. Or the North London. Wherever they can fit me in. I want us all to be together for one last time. You, Annabelle. Toby if Annabelle wants him there. And I want to say goodbye properly to everyone. And know when I've got all my wits about me. This is it. This is the end for us. And we know. We know where we are. Everyone knows if you don't say this. Or that. Now. That's it.

Julie We? What you saying, Alf?

Alfie Once I've gone into the hospice I want to be on my own.

Julie *covers her mouth involuntarily. Silence.*

Alfie I thought maybe this next one. When they bring me in. In to the church.

Alfie *finds another song and presses play on his iPhone.*

'My Lover's Prayer' by Otis Redding plays. They listen to a bit, look at each other.

Julie Alfie –

Alfie *immediately switches it off.*

Alfie I associate it with Mum. She loved soul music. Loved a crooner. Sam Cooke. Nat King Cole. Otis.

Julie I know.

Alfie I've kind of got this mad idea. You know? Of it playing. And it's like. I'm coming home, Mum.

Julie Alf –

Alfie I want to be buried in my Chipie dungarees and my Kickers.

Julie What?

Alfie It's all in that vacuum pack in the loft. It'll all fit me again now . . .

Julie Alf, babe . . .

Alfie I don't even know why I'm even saying all this. I don't want a funeral.

Julie You what?

Alfie I don't like the idea. I want to say goodbye while I've got all my wits about me. And I'm not too weak. And that's it. Throw a party a month or two later. I'm sure one of my mates will play some records.

Julie Don't you want me to hold your hand? Don't you think I want to hold your hand?

Alfie I can't think of anything worse than us fading out. Me all drugged up. Except maybe I can still hear a bit. The sound of you and Annabelle. Crying.

Julie We won't.

Alfie Hearing you suffering.

Julie I promise you we won't. We're strong, babe, we're strong.

Alfie It's my worst fear.

Julie I will give you everything to comfort you. And calm you. And love you.

Alfie I'd rather be on my own at the End.

Julie This isn't right, Alf. What about me and Annabelle? What about me and Annabelle?

Alfie It's best for all of us.

Julie It's not.

Alfie It is.

Julie You're only thinking of one person here. And it's not me and it's not Annabelle.

Alfie I know I don't deserve you.

Julie Why are you doing this?

Silence.

The night we got together in Daniels. You said 'do you believe in love at first sight?' And I said, yes. And you got hold of my hand. And you said. That's it now, babe. I'm never letting go . . .

Alfie What a nutty little club.

Julie You looked so pure.

Alfie Baby face.

Julie And I had no idea you were such a thug when you went to football.

Alfie I can't think of anything lonelier. Than watching you, watching me go. The last things I hear is your voice quivering. Like it does when I know that great big heart's gonna break. We'll be together again one day.

Julie We won't. Don't talk nonsense, Alf. This is it.

Silence.

I've known you since I was twenty-three years of age. And we haven't had no religious crap once. Don't start now. This is it.

Alfie Please, Julie.

Julie What about me? What about Annabelle? For crying out loud, Alfie. There's something going on here. I'm not stupid.

Julie *goes into the kitchen and boils the kettle.*

She makes a pot of tea and brings it in, finding a heatproof mat before she puts it on the dining table.

It's an elegant old china teapot, at odds with the rest of their taste.

Alfie I'm glad me and Annabelle got over to West Ham to see the last one.

Julie It meant a lot to her.

Alfie I wish we'd gone to football together a bit more often.

Julie She enjoyed going over with you when she went.

Alfie It's hard to believe this time next year we'll have done our first season in the Olympic stadium. It was so depressing when Man U went two-one up. It was like, this is so West Ham. There's gonna be no happy ending here.

Julie No.

Alfie And then. Bosh. Payet floats it in and Michail Antonio's up like a salmon. And it's in the net. Goal. Quarter of an hour to go. Valencia concedes the free kick. It's Payet again.

Perfect. Winston Reid. He's not up like a salmon.

Julie *laughs.*

Alfie But he gets his nut on it. Goal!

Alfie *celebrates like a Brazilian football commentator, waving his walking stick in the air.*

Alfie   GOOOOOOOOOOOOOOOOOAAAAAAAAAAAAAAAAAAAAAALLLLLLL! GOOOOOOOOOOOAAAAAAAAAAAAAALLLLLLLLLLLLLLLLLLLLLLLLLL! WINSTON-REIIIIIIIIIIIIIIIIIIIIIIIIIIIIIIIIIIIIIIIID! WINNNNNNNNNNNSTON REID GOOOOOOOOOOOOOOOAAAAAAAAAAAAAAAAAALLLLLLLLLLL! BELO! BELO! BELO!

Alfie *laughs,* **Julie** *laughs.*

Julie   Do you really want to be on your own?

Silence.

Alfie   Ten minutes to go. Kouyaté has a pop. Five minutes go. Ref checks his watch. Five minutes on the board. Another five minutes. We're all whistling. Come on, ref! And then he blows up. He blows up. We've done Man U. We've won. We've won. Our last ever game at Upton Park. Everyone was going nuts. And me and Annabelle are hanging onto each other for dear life. Laughing and crying. Laughing and crying. When we walked up Green Street towards the tube. She held my hand like she was eight years old again. It's funny to think it was the last time we'll ever do that. Somehow knowing it was the last time for everyone takes the edge off. I do understand what it is I'm asking.

Julie   I don't know what Annabelle's going to say.

Silence.

Alfie   It's a bit weird to think we'll be in the Olympic Stadium next season and I won't be going.

Julie   I reckon you'll be alright to go to the first one.

Alfie   I won't. I'll be on the way out by then.

Julie   I loved the Olympics.

Alfie   I'll never forget Mo winning that ten thousand metres.

Julie It was magic.

Alfie That little look over his shoulder. Just to make sure.

Julie I've been thinking of writing a novel set over that summer.

Alfie Have you, babe?

Julie Yeah, yeah, I've been thinking about for a while.

Alfie Great.

Julie It's been a bit hard to commit to it. You know? While there's been so much uncertainty.

Alfie I'm sorry.

Julie It's not your fault.

Alfie I sometimes feel like it is.

Julie It's not.

Alfie I've not exactly had the healthiest lifestyle.

Julie It's just cancer. The cunt.

Silence.

Alfie Have you got a story?

Julie I like that Michael Cunningham novel. The one that was turned into a film. The one that was riffing off *Mrs Dalloway*.

Alfie You thinking of doing something a bit more arty?

Julie The thought of writing another crime book actually bores me to tears.

Alfie You go for it, darling.

Julie I think I'm going to write under a different name.

Alfie Really?

Julie Yeah. I can't put that novel out under my name. I'm in a box with Martina Cole as it is. I'll be patronised to fuck.

Alfie What is it?

Julie What? The novel?

Alfie Yeah.

Julie Ordinary people. Little earthquakes in their lives. The opening ceremony. The hundred metres final. The closing ceremony. I'm imagining it's quite stream of consciousness. I really want to write like that. Write normal people like us. Like that. My agent's going to lose her shit. All she'll be able to see is me pushing pound notes down the drain.

Alfie Don't worry about her . . .

Julie She'll be alright. She'll have to be.

Alfie It's a long time since we've been ordinary people.

Julie Where you're from never leaves you. Not really. Does it, Alf?

Alfie Perhaps you'll get going on your book before Christmas?

Julie There's another book I want to do first.

Alfie Blimey, what's that one? There's another one?

Silence.

Julie I loved that the summer. The Olympics. Everything felt so hopeful.

Alfie Will you do what I want?

Julie Don't you think we need a new approach, Alf? Maybe we need to look abroad. Go down a more integrative route . . .

Alfie Abroad where?

Julie I know the chemo's brutal so maybe we need something less toxic . . .

Alfie Like what?

Julie I've been looking and looking and looking on Google and there's a whole world out there. It goes far beyond what Dr Chan and Mr Rahman have put on the table, babe.

These people abroad. They harness the power existing inside all of us. That's inside our bodies already. It's Metabolic, Alf. You detoxify. They strengthen your immune system. And then they go after the cancer with organic, natural chemicals. The drug's called Laetrile. There's this clinic I've found that'll suit us down to the ground.

Alfie And how much is all this going to cost?

Julie Fifty grand. Ish.

Alfie Fifty grand?

Julie That's what our rainy day money's for, Alfie.

Alfie That's for Annabelle when we're gone . . .

Julie Annabelle will want her dad to be around.

Alfie Where is it?

Julie Tijuana.

Alfie Tijuana?

Julie Yeah.

Alfie The last time I went to Tijuana I was held hostage for twelve hours by a Cartel who had a beef with the promoter of the rave. I had all me records nicked and I never got paid. No thanks, babe.

Julie These people are curing people. Their scans are clean Alf. We've got so much more to come.

Silence.

Year after next we've both got our big birthday, haven't we? The big six-o. That is our year, babe. We've got to get you well. We've got to have our party. The Earl Haig in Crouch

End. That's perfect that is. They'll let us have the whole place to ourselves. Get one hundred and fifty in there easy. We'll have a really good do. And we've got to go on our holidays. It's always been a dream of mine since I was a little girl to go to Hawaii.

Waikiki Beach and a little bit of Hula-Hula. And I know you want to walk the Dolomites.

Alfie Walk the Dolomites?

Julie All the beautiful meadows of the South Tyrol. The Lake at Misurina. Lunch at the Larieto.

Alfie I could no more walk the Dolomites than I could walk down to Green Lanes to nip into Tesco.

Julie There'll come a day when we're both thinning out so much on top we'll cut our hair. Start looking the same. Matching gilets. And a National Trust membership. Pottering round Chartwell. Holding hands. And never letting go.

Alfie Ju . . .

Julie *composes herself.*

Julie I'd like us to make more of the Garden. D'you remember when we had your Studio constructed the builder was talking about the soil. The moist soil in north London. I did some finding out at the time. But I never did nothing about it. You didn't seem too interested, Alf. It's moist. It suits the Perennials. Himalayan Honeysuckle and Michaelmas Daisy. We could have a little vegetable garden. Cabbage and Cauli. Home-grown stick of celery. Our own compost heap. Rake up the leaves when the season's on the turn.

Alfie I won't see sixty.

Julie You might.

Alfie I won't see seventy.

Julie You will if you want to.

Silence.

Alfie You honestly think two enemas a day, a load of raw carrot juice and a Laetrile infusion will cure me? Do you know what Laetrile is, babe? It breaks down into cyanide. It's more toxic than any chemo I've ever had. That's right. I've had my moments in the middle of the night grasping at straws.

Julie *cries briefly but just as quickly sits on all of it, all the feeling and hurt.*

Alfie Writers don't retire any more than DJs do, do they, babe?

Julie No.

Alfie One day they just stop. Let's not string things out. Don't string it out, let's all say goodbye properly. And then you can leave me to it. In the hospital. Or the hospice. Or wherever I am. I'll be alright.

Julie I won't be.

Alfie I'll have all my memories. And I'll think about you throwing a great big party for me when it's not such a sad time. I can look at my phone.

Julie You can look at your phone?

Alfie As long as I can still pick it up.

Julie It's so selfish, Alfie. It's so fucking selfish.

Alfie I've reached the end of the road, babe . . .

Julie You haven't. Alright. You won't go abroad. But you heard Dr Chan. He said they'd had a big talk about options at the Tumour Board. Mr Rahman said he's happy to go again. If we go down that road. And Dr Chan might get you on a trial.

Alfie But I don't want that, babe.

Julie I don't want you to go.

Alfie This is it, babe. Tell me what you want. What do you want?

Julie I want you home.

Alfie Home?

Julie I want you here.

Julie *looks around the room, thinks.*

Alfie In here?

Julie Yeah.

Alfie In a bed down here?

Alfie *looks around the room, thinks.*

Julie Are you hungry?

Alfie No.

Julie I can mash up a bit of banana and a kiwi fruit with some yoghurt?

Alfie I told you I'm not hungry.

Julie At least let me give you a funeral.

They look at each other for as long as you think you can get away with.

Julie You want that Otis Redding song on the way in?

Alfie I don't know, Ju . . .

Julie And one of your favourites on the way out.

Alfie Maybe.

Julie Can I pick one? Am I allowed?

Alfie You want to pick one?

Julie Yeah. And?

Julie *smiles,* **Alfie** *laughs and offers his phone.*

Julie *goes to* **Alfie** *and takes his phone. She starts to scroll through his iMusic app. She finds the track she's looking for. She looks at* **Alfie**.

Julie   You were the first person I ever heard play this record.

Alfie   Well I don't know what it is yet?

Julie   I was at home with Annabelle. And you had that spot on Centreforce. And Rodney T had just handed over to you. And you were, like. 'Keep it locked London. Here we go. House music all night long.'

Alfie *laughs. 'Your Love' by Frankie Knuckles plays.*

Julie *dances,* **Alfie** *nods his head, enjoying watching her dance. She's a really good dancer, sexy, confident, funny, full of life.*

Julie *realises that it's becoming painful for* **Alfie** *watching her. She stops dancing, and it all becomes much too much for him and he turns away from her. Silence.*

Julie *switches off the music.* **Alfie** *turns back. She goes to him and kisses him, passionately. He lets his hands linger on her bottom.*

Julie *smiles and takes* **Alfie** *by the hand and guides him to the sofa. She takes his walking stick and puts it down.*

Julie *kisses* **Alfie** *and takes his shorts off and has a look at his penis.*

Julie   Going commando I see.

Alfie   Always ready for you, babe.

Julie *laughs, stands and pulls down her knickers which she throws. And then she gently straddles* **Alfie**, *kissing him and moving gently against him.*

Alfie *wants to enter her and she helps him and they begin to very gently and beautifully make love. It's been a while and quite quickly he orgasms.*

Julie *holds him,* **Alfie** *holds her. They cling onto each other for dear life. They look at each other for as long as you think you can get away with.*

Julie You okay?

Alfie Yeah.

She kisses him, lifts herself off of **Alfie** *and heads over to a box of tissues, before cleaning herself up quickly in the kitchen and washing her hands. Silence.*

Julie *comes back in with some kind of emollient cream. She looks at* **Alfie** *and fetches more tissues.*

Alfie I want to touch you.

Julie It's okay.

Alfie Please.

Julie I'm gasping for a cup of tea.

Alfie Thanks a bunch.

Julie Hold me.

Alfie *nods and* **Julie** *sits next to him on the sofa. They hug, look at each other and* **Julie** *thinks.*

Julie *wipes* **Alfie** *with the tissues and dresses him with the clothes she brought down for him. She uses the emollient cream to soothe his feet and hands.*

She's tender and careful, sensitive to his frailty. She puts the tissues in her pocket. She finds his Sliders.

Alfie Help me up.

Julie Aren't you tired?

Alfie I don't want to sit down. I'll get all locked up.

Julie That tea's gone cold.

Julie *helps* **Alfie** *up. He's a bit unsteady and gestures for his walking stick, which* **Julie** *passes to him. He's in comfortable branded clothes, joggers and a tee-shirt.*

Julie *passes* **Alfie** *his phone, which had fallen out of his pocket on to the sofa. She goes to the teapot and* **Alfie** *watches her.*

Alfie That was the last time wasn't it?

Silence.

Julie It better not be, I didn't get my oats!

Julie *laughs.*

Alfie I think maybe it was.

Julie Don't be daft.

Alfie *laughs and shakes his head.*

Alfie I'm sorry it was so quick . . .

Julie Alf, honestly . . .

Alfie But for me it was lovely. You are lovely. The way you were looking at me . . .

Julie Don't, Alfie, you'll make me cry . . . Annabelle's coming.

Alfie I'm so lucky you didn't walk out on me.

Julie Don't go there. Don't go there. There's no need.

Alfie We'd spent years talking about getting married.

Silence.

I think I got what I deserved with cancer.

Silence.

Julie What's going on, Alfie? Come on. Our relationship has always been based on complete and total honesty. Apart from the time you fucked your Tour Manager for six months behind my back.

Silence.

Alfie You don't sound like you've ever forgiven me?

Julie Why on earth are you bringing all this up? This is about us now.

Alfie I know. But.

Julie Don't you know how broken I am inside, Alf? This is the last thing I want to talk about now.

Julie *looks for her phone, which she's left charging downstairs overnight. She looks at it briefly and then puts it in her dress pocket.*

Julie *looks at him, thinks.*

Alfie She wants to see me.

Julie What?

Alfie She does. She wants to see me.

Julie Her?

Alfie She heard I'm not well again and she wants to see me.

Julie No.

Alfie That's what I said.

Julie No.

Alfie I felt sick when I saw her email.

Julie She sent you an email did she? Can I see it?

Julie Can I see it, Alf?

Alfie I deleted it, Ju. And I deleted my reply. It made me feel sick.

Julie Is that because you didn't want me to see them?

Alfie I don't want nothing to do with her.

Julie What did you say?

Alfie I told her the past's in the past. I told her you wouldn't want it. I told her not to contact me again.

Julie But is that what you want?

Alfie What?

Julie You told her I wouldn't want you to see her.

Alfie Yeah?

Julie What about you?

Silence.

Well there's my answer.

Alfie I don't, Ju.

Julie This is what all this shit's about.

Alfie It's not.

Julie When did she send you this email?

Alfie Three weeks ago.

Julie Three weeks ago? Three fucking weeks ago and you haven't said shit?

Alfie I knew you'd react.

Julie Well what did you think I was going to do? Hang out the bunting? You shit on me. And if that wasn't enough ten years down the road you've flushed me down the toilet.

Silence.

You think after all these years I don't know you?

Alfie Course I don't.

Julie Is this what all this is about?

Alfie No. Honest. It isn't.

Julie You can't see both of us, you can't have a proper goodbye from both of us, so you won't have none of us.

Alfie My wishes have got nothing to do with her!

Julie Haven't they?

Alfie I don't want nothing to do with her. I've not heard a word from her or seen her in ten years. I don't want to see her. It made me feel like shit.

Julie And now you've made me feel like shit.

Alfie Good riddance to bad rubbish. That's all I am.

Silence.

Julie I don't buy this.

Alfie If you don't believe me have a read. They're in the bin in my old Hotmail.

Alfie *offers* **Julie** *his phone. She hesitates.*

Alfie *offers his phone and* **Julie** *takes it. She finds the emails. It takes the time it takes for her to read them.* **Alfie** *watches her.*

Julie She says here 'I will always love you'. But you don't say nothing about your feelings. Nothing.

Silence.

Did you love her?

Alfie What does it matter?

Julie You told me it was only a shag . . .

Alfie Ju . . .

Julie You did then? You loved her?

Alfie All that matters is we survived. I never, ever stopped loving you. Ever. But do you think I'm the sort of arsehole who'd be in that situation and not feel nothing?

Silence.

There. Is that better or worse? What good has that done?

Julie There ain't no absolution without the truth first, Alf.

Alfie I was a fool. I didn't say nothing inappropriate. Or false. Or nothing you or me could be ashamed of. Being honest. I did wonder if I'd bump in to her some time. Randomly. At some gig. On the street. In an airport lounge. But when I clicked send. I knew that was it. It's final. This is it. Everything's for the last time now.

Julie *moves towards him, he puts his hands up but she persists and returns his phone.*

Julie *moves away, she hesitates, thinks.*

Julie I've got something to tell you. I need to speak. I need to tell you things. There's things I need to say.

Alfie You can say whatever you want.

Julie Can I?

Alfie Course you can.

Julie I'm frightened as well.

Alfie Of what?

Julie Of how you'll react.

Alfie Just say it, it's okay.

Julie I want to write about us.

Alfie Us?

Julie Yes, us.

Alfie What?

Julie I really thought the Olympics book was going to be the next one . . .

Alfie Right.

Julie But all I can think about is us.

Alfie Right?

Julie And you.

Alfie Me?

Julie And what you're going through . . .

Alfie Right.

Julie And what we're going through and what Annabelle's going through . . . What we're going through as a family.

Alfie Right.

Julie Are you okay?

Alfie I'm fine.

Julie Are you okay for me to tell you this?

Alfie I said, I'm fine.

Julie I'd begun to shape it all in my head like a book . . .

Alfie What?

Julie If I tell myself the story. When it started. The fork in the road. Imagining how it will all turn out in the end. It's a way of reassuring myself I'll get through. Somehow I'll manage.

Silence.

In the last five years. Ever since we first heard the C word out loud. I must have told myself the story of our whole relationship a thousand times in my head. And it's started to organise itself into chapters. One. Nineteen eighty-one. A funny little night club over Hornchurch Bus Garage. Girl meets boy. Two. Two thousand and eleven. Blood. Diagnosis. Three. Back in time. Nineteen eighty-three. DJ Froggy helper. I can't help it. As the months have gone by I've realised I actually. Really. Want to write it. I'm going to write it.

Alfie You wouldn't, would you?

Julie Listen to me.

Alfie Okay.

Julie Nineteen eighty-seven. Our first holiday on The Island. Annabelle was only four wasn't she, Alf? And you went to see Alfredo play and to find out what all the fuss was about.

And you come home at ten o'clock in the morning. Gurning like a goldfish. 'You've got to go Amnesia, Ju, you've got to go, babe'. And the next night you stopped in with Annabel and I went. And I had my first E. And I danced on the terrace until the sun came up. And when I walked back to the apartment I reflected. How brilliant it was you'd had your good time. And then you made sure I could go out and have my good time.

Silence.

The life we've had, Alf. We've done so much. We've been through so much together. Ten years ago you sent an email meant for her to me. And I became a completely different person. Like that.

Julie *clicks her fingers.*

Julie Vengeful, angry. Sometimes consumed by rage.

Alfie Well I never saw that side of you once . . .

Julie I didn't want you to see that me.

Alfie You what?

Julie So I didn't show you. I 'did' instead.

Alfie You did? What did you do, Ju?

Silence.

Julie I told your mum and dad what you'd done.

Alfie You told my mum what I'd done?

Julie *nods. They consider each other.*

Julie I went round to see them. I could see the shame on your dad's face. He sunk back into his armchair. Gripping the arms on it as if he was taking off on an aeroplane.

Alfie What did you do that for?

Julie Your mum made a pot of tea and got the biscuit tin out. She was lovely. It was the only time she was ever nice to me. Though of course she still made it my fault you'd 'dallied'. 'Dallied.' Blaming it on me doing my MA.

Alfie Mum knew?

Julie Yeah, I told them.

Alfie She never said nothing to me about it once.

Julie You was always on a pedestal, Alf.

Alfie Oh my God. What did you do that for?

Silence.

Julie I was hurting bad, Alf. I had an inkling it would never be mentioned again. And once I'd got it off my chest I could try and rebuild myself. And our relationship.

Silence.

I appreciated you stopped touring. I didn't want to seem ungrateful but honestly, Alf . . .

When you was away all the time. I could write at the weekends. I could write after Annabelle went to bed.

When Annabelle was a teenager and went to uni I had even more space. But then you was in my face. And I had another two Karen David books to write. And all the pleasure in writing was gone.

Silence.

It was hard. That time was hard. But we got through it. And we've had a brilliant life together. You still make me laugh.

Silence.

But you see if I don't write it down, Alf. The good and the bad and the indifferent. Everything. It'll all be lost. Everything. Not just you. Everything. You can't leave me on my own without that book.

Alfie Is that why you want to be with me?

Julie What?

Alfie So you can write about me dying.

Julie *composes herself.*

Julie No, that's not fair.

Alfie I'll tell you what's not fair. Knowing you'll never walk your daughter up the aisle on her wedding day. Or play that cheesy old Bros record she loved when she was a kid for her first dance. And come out from behind the decks and lead your partner onto the dancefloor to join her and your son-in-law.

Silence.

Alfie I'll tell you what's not fair. Knowing if your daughter ever has children you'll never watch them bounce up and down on a trampoline in your back garden. That's what's not fair. There. Put that in your fucking book.

Julie Please. Annabelle's coming.

Silence.

Alfie I'm sorry for my anger.

Julie Don't you dare.

Alfie Ju?

Silence.

Julie Why don't I make a fresh pot and why don't we go and have it in the garden?

Alfie I can't be bothered with the garden.

Julie It's such a beautiful morning, Alf . . .

Alfie I'm tired.

Julie Sit down love.

Alfie If I sit down I won't get back up again.

Julie Why don't you go in The Studio?

Alfie It will make me feel depressed.

Julie Is there football on later?

Alfie I'm not fussed today.

Julie When are England playing again?

Alfie Tomorrow.

Julie Who are we playing?

Alfie Slovakia.

Julie D'you think we'll win?

Alfie Honestly, Julie, I don't know.

Julie I hope he doesn't pick that butterfingers in goal again.

Alfie You don't have to make pointless conversation.

Julie It's not pointless conversation.

Alfie What is it then?

Julie I want you to fight.

Alfie What, fight for more radiotherapy? And chemo? That won't even work.

Julie It might . . .

Alfie And miracle of miracles it does work, surgery that might kill me anyway. And lucky me, if I get through the operation. I'm a bloated husk with a colostomy bag. I want to go with a bit of dignity thanks very much.

Julie But we might get another year?

Alfie Might.

Julie Yes.

Alfie And I might also turn out for Roy Hodgson tomorrow instead of Wayne Rooney.

Silence.

Julie Don't you want to live?

Alfie Of course I want to.

Julie Then try!

Alfie I'm dying, Ju!

Julie Do it for me, do it for Annabelle!

Alfie I'm dying!

Julie Do it for us!

Alfie This is cruel.

Julie How can it be cruel wanting you to live?

Alfie *and* **Julie** *look at each other. They look at each other for as long as you think you can get away with.*

Alfie I've had my time, it's okay.

Julie It's not over . . .

Alfie I've got some regrets . . .

Julie What regrets?

Alfie I wish I'd got sober before I got ill.

Silence.

I wish I'd taken my own music more seriously. Put more records out.

Silence.

The things I've seen. In the club. People are ugly, normal, off their heads. You see magical first kisses. Couples breaking up on the dancefloor. I've seen two heart attacks and a stroke. Fella literally died in the club. And we never even switched the music off and put the lights on. There's always one trainspotter standing at the front. You think to yourself. Is he enjoying himself? There's always one angry bloke in the crowd who catches your eye and shows you his middle finger.

Julie There's always one angry bloke . . .

Alfie *laughs, thinks.*

Alfie I keep thinking about that spot I had for a bit at the Berwick. I had a white label of that Joey Beltram record. 'Energy Flash'. As soon as the Berwick hears it they know it's special, right? That hard, nine-o-nine kick. The high hat's driving everything forwards.

Maybe because it was near home. I identified with the kids dancing in front of the booth. Like I used to. Watching Froggy at the Ilford Town Hall Junior Disco every Monday.

Anyway these kids. One of them had a French Crop and he was totally off of his head. And there was another one who had an haircut like Clint Boon. And he was gurning like a motherfucker. And the last one. Was this kid with a classic raver's bob. He was so fresh-faced I don't know how he ever got let in there! They looked fucking funny the three of them. And they caught my eye as I smiled at them and they were having such a great time. Dancing, just dancing. No one was thinking about anything. Except the simple and immense pleasure of the moment.

Silence.

When that record drops, the pyro goes off, and the smoke's flying through the arms in the air. There's nothing like it. I used to think what I did for a living was trivial. And what you did was important. All those years you spent teaching. Creating books that can last. But I've come round to believing maybe creating fleeting moments of joy in this dark world actually matters.

Silence.

I've had my time, it's okay. I don't even know if I'd want to be part of the scene now.

Who wants to be on a bill as long as your arm and play an hour-long set? I can't tell a story in an hour. I want it be epic. I want four hours. Five hours. I want to transcend genre. I want to play house, old school, I want to play fresh music, acid, drum and base, northern soul, rare groove, techno, hardcore, disco, garage. I want to play afrobeat one minute and then go bananas with the 'Theme to the Dambusters'. I want to play for people who want to dance and sweat.

Silence.

But the world's moved on, eh Ju? I'm useless. I'm fucked. But you dancing earlier . . . And I didn't have the strength to join in.

Silence.

Alfie When the time comes. Let me crawl into a corner. Cats have got the right idea. Find a quiet spot on their own and go to sleep.

Julie It's a myth.

Alfie What is?

Julie It's a fairy tale to make us feel better. They're old or sick. Or both. Maybe disoriented and can't find their way back home. They don't know where they are and they're lonely. And they give up. That's all it is.

Alfie Is it?

Julie Alfie, you've got the privilege of musing over the past. Being in the now. You won't be here tomorrow. But I will.

Alfie *nods.*

Alfie I can't do this anymore.

Alfie *gingerly heads into the kitchen out through the back door into the garden. He slams the back door shut as he goes.* **Julie** *is alone. Silence.*

Julie *goes into the kitchen and gets out some plates, bread, ketchup, mayonnaise, HP Sauce, butter and some cutlery, which she brings in and puts on the dining table.*

Julie *notices the teapot. She picks it up and feels it. It's stone cold. She tries to compose herself and closes her eyes.*

She walks in the room. She lets the teapot fall and it smashes on the floor. Broken china and tea go everywhere. She looks at the mess. Silence.

She gets down on her knees and lies on the floor in a foetal position, trying with all her might to keep everything in.

She can't. She screams, voicing all her anguish and pain. Silence.

Alfie *comes back in.* **Julie** *becomes self-conscious and sits up.*

Alfie What's happened here?

They look at the mess, the broken china.

Julie Nana Vi's teapot survived the Blitz, Uncle Peter setting the house in Poole Road on fire during the three-day week and I was hoping it might see off Vote Leave. And as for that David-fucking-Cameron?

Julie *goes into the kitchen.*

Alfie *looks at the mess. He's upset. She fetches a cloth and a dustpan and brush and begins to clear up.*

Julie I feel like everything's going backwards. The teapot's been another thing.

All the broken china and tea bags go in the bin.

She fetches a bucket of cold water and detergent and washes the floor. It takes the time it takes.

Alfie I don't like to see you like that . . .

Julie What?

Alfie It's as if I can see you here on your own.

Julie *absorbs this and continues cleaning up. She thinks.*

Julie   I imagine after the apocalypse we'd have tea. A pot of tea. Me, Annabelle, Toby.

Alfie   Tea?

Julie   There'd be Gail's sourdough and some custard creams. Maybe we'd open a bottle of white wine. And we'd fall about laughing watching Toby struggle with the cork. Toast your memory.

Julie *gets up, looks at* **Alfie***. She takes the bucket, cloth and dustpan and brush back into the kitchen.*

Julie *looks at her phone and replies to a WhatsApp. They look at each other, think.*

Julie   Annabelle said she'll be another half an hour. Did you go in the Studio?

Alfie   No, I was only out there a minute. I fancied a vape.

Julie   A vape?

Alfie   But Chris next door was giving Tina one. And he'd left the window open.

Julie   Oh God.

Alfie   It was like he was on the final furlong of the Grand National . . .

Julie   You what?

Alfie   'That's it. That's it. Good girl. There's a good girl.'

Julie   'There's a good girl?'

Alfie   There am I reflecting upon the meaning of existence. And Chris next door is making me reconsider afresh what it is to make sweet love to a woman.

Silence.

Julie   I do want you to consider the options with Dr Chan.

Alfie Ju, babe, please . . .

Julie Alfie, please listen . . . You've got to let me say this . . . You and your dad didn't express no emotions. All you ever did was talk about work, and West Ham and what Annabelle had been up to. I can't imagine how agonising it is, babe. But I promise you it won't be grim. We won't do any howling and crying or anything like that. We'll do what we've always done as a family. Have a laugh. And pull each other's legs.

Alfie But I don't want no more chemo. I can't take any more. I haven't got it in me.

Julie Well we'd make the best of it.

Alfie Well what would we do?

Julie We'd try and get out and about a bit while you've got the energy.

Alfie Where?

Julie We could get down to Rye maybe.

Alfie This is hard.

Julie To Whitstable. Bag of chips. Looking at the sea.

Alfie What else?

Julie We can talk. Talk about anything and everything. We can play Shithead. We can listen to music and reminisce.

Alfie Right.

Julie Maybe if you're feeling up to it we can go to bed. And have a cuddle again.

Silence.

We'll go and vote next Thursday. We'll watch the Euros. Hopefully England will do alright. If you wanted we could go down to have a look at Upton Park before they demolish the stadium. Go in the Pie and Mash on Barking Road. Maybe you could help me with my book?

Alfie What?

Julie Maybe we could do it together . . . It would be something for Annabelle. It would be something for the grandchildren.

Alfie We ain't got no grandchildren.

Silence.

Julie You could tell me what you want. We could talk when you've got the energy. And then when you're resting I would write.

Alfie You do what you like. You hang out all our dirty washing . . .

Julie It hurts you don't trust me, Alf. After everything we've been through. All these years. And I've never let you down once. Not once.

Alfie It's so obvious now it's come to it you've never, ever, forgiven me.

Julie I could have started again. Annabelle had gone to uni.

Alfie I'm sorry, I'm so sorry I did it . . .

Julie I wanted to cut your fucking dick off.

Alfie Well Ju, that's understandable.

Julie Alfie love, I accepted it a long time ago. I decided to put it to the back of my mind as much as I could. A long time ago. Sometimes I thought there was something wrong with me.

Alfie Does Annabelle know? Does she?

Julie She'd never have forgiven us if I'd told her. You, for doing what you did. And me, for telling her.

Silence.

You were the love of my life. You are the love of my life. How could I ever forgive you?

Alfie You're the love of my life.

Julie It's done now. Look at me. It's done.

Silence.

Alfie Why do you want to write about us?

Julie It's okay, I won't do it.

Silence.

Alfie I've read all the stuff in the papers. I know what you've said about your writing. But why would you write about us?

Silence.

Julie When I was a kid I wrote things all the time. I had a secret journal with a padlock. All I did was write down what had happened. Literally. Like when Mum's cat Bobby was run over by the Bin Man. The pleasure I took in describing his crushed hind legs was quite weird. I always wrote stories. But as I got older. It changed. I was a bit ashamed of what I wrote. About my mates, and boys. And Mum and Dad. I wrote down their rows. She didn't think Dad was enough for her.

Silence.

Mum used to find the exercise books I wrote in. And she went absolutely berserk. She ripped them up. She used to scream. 'Don't you think you can write down private things about me and your dad, you little bitch.'

Silence.

I've been writing about my mum my whole life, Alfie babe. Trying to understand her. Where do you think D.I. Karen Davis, the Queen of Romford nick comes from? But I don't literally write my mum.

Silence.

I don't mean to sound callous but I was never much interested in writing about your family. They were so ordinary.

Silence.

I like the feeling when the books come out. I can have an effect on people. It's addictive. After a while I realised I could make people laugh as well. I'm never quick-witted enough in real life. Am I?

Alfie You make me laugh.

Julie I like impressing people. I wasn't a bad teacher but writing . . . When I started to really take it seriously I like impressing you. I like watching you read a manuscript. Pulling a face when something unexpected. Or naughty happens in the story. Don't tell me that's never going to happen again.

Julie *wants to cry. Doesn't.*

Alfie Do I deserve you? Have I ever deserved you?

He walks in the room.

Alfie Tell the truth in your book. I don't want no hogwash. I don't want people thinking I was some beige wanker.

Julie People don't think you're beige, babe. They've only got to go on YouTube. That video of you at Raindance is really something quite special.

Alfie That is thirty seconds of infamy that is.

Julie It is.

Alfie That's a one-man advert that is. For why it's not good to consume two grams of Charlie, six Doves and a Purple Ohm.

Julie *laughs.* **Alfie** *laughs. Silence.*

Alfie You know everything. You can write a perfect book.

Julie I don't know about that.

Alfie Will you help me talk to Annabelle?

Julie Annabelle's pregnant.

Alfie What?

Julie You know. Pregnant.

Julie *makes a pregnant belly gesture and smiles.*

Alfie She's what?

Julie She did the test last week.

Alfie What?

Julie I think she did about three. One after the other.

Alfie She's pregnant?

Julie Yeah.

Alfie Why didn't you tell me? Did Annabelle ask you not to tell me?

Silence.

Julie The baby's due beginning-middle of February.

Alfie *lets his walking stick fall. They look at the walking stick.*

Alfie I'm alright, Ju. It's lovely news. I'm over the moon.

Alfie *looks at his walking stick and gingerly gets down on one knee to pick it up.*

Julie *goes to him and helps him back up.*

Julie It's okay.

Alfie I'm alright, I'm alright.

Julie You don't have to be.

Alfie Well I'll know to rearrange my face when she tells me.

Silence.

Annabelle, blimey, out of wedlock.

Julie Didn't have Annabelle up the duff on my Annabelle bingo card. Did you?

Alfie No.

Silence.

Julie I loved those summers on The Island.

Alfie When Annabelle was little?

Julie Yeah.

Alfie Me too.

Silence.

What are you going to do when I'm gone? What are you really going to do?

Julie I don't want to talk about it, Alf babe.

Alfie Annabelle will need help, won't she? She'll need help with the baby. When the baby comes. Won't she, Ju?

Julie I don't want to talk about it now.

Silence.

Alfie You need to get on with your life, Julie.

Julie I honestly don't know.

Alfie You should get yourself on a cruise. The ones they do for single people.

Julie Alf . . .

Alfie Just be careful. Two weeks in the Caribbean on the Azura and that's a lot of silver surfers with a touch of the itchy ball sack.

Julie *laughs.* **Alfie** *laughs.*

Julie The idea of another body is . . .

Alfie Probably quite appealing.

Julie You couldn't be more wrong. I've only ever wanted you.

Alfie You could get yourself a dog. It will be some company. See your mates. Do things you enjoy. Go out dancing.

Julie I'm too old to go out dancing.

Alfie Drop a couple of Benny's. Bosh. Have it. You're a fantastic dancer.

Julie I don't want you to go.

Alfie You'll be alright. You will. Everything will be alright in the end.

Julie The only certainty I've got is Annabelle. And my work.

Alfie What do you imagine? What's in your head? What's your day like?

Julie I can't Alf . . .

Alfie Go on. You can do it.

Julie Erm. Listening to Radio Four in the morning. *The Today Programme*. Tea and toast with marmalade in bed. The house is quiet. A walk. To clear my head and think about the book. Maybe a loop of Ally Pally. Or a walk over to Crouch End. One day over the railway track at Harringay. The next day over Hornsey. Perhaps a coffee in Gail's with my notebook. Gawp at all the Crouch End types. And ear-wig their pretensions. And fail completely to acknowledge I am one of them. And have been for a long time.

Alfie You know what you could do, Ju?

Julie What?

Alfie You could turn the Studio into your office.

Julie I couldn't do that . . .

End   215

Alfie   It's yours.

Julie   I couldn't . . .

Alfie   I want you to.

Julie   What am I going to with all your vinyl?

Alfie   See what Annabelle wants. And sell the rest.

Julie   To who?

Alfie   There'll be a hundred and one vinyl junkies all over it. You won't have no trouble.

Julie   It's too hard after everything . . .

Alfie   It's not. You're strong. You're the strongest person I know.

Julie   Am I?

Alfie   You can write in the Studio. Put a wood burner in there. A dog basket under your desk. For the puppy. In the summer work with the doors open. Like I did.

Julie   Could I?

Alfie   All your writer mates will be well jealous. You'll have the biggest shed of the lot.

They look at each other for as long as you think you can get away with.

Julie   Now you know about Annabelle, are you sure, Alf?

Silence.

You don't have to decide anything now.

Silence.

But you might feel different when you wake up tomorrow? You might feel different after you've seen Annabelle? Don't you think Annabelle might want to be with you?

Especially now what with her news.

Alfie *feels agitated and walks in the room a touch.*

Julie She's going to be devastated when we tell her you don't want no more treatment. But if we can tell her that we're looking at options. Perhaps February's unrealistic . . . But perhaps. Perhaps. If you could experience feeling the baby kick in Annabelle's tummy. Put your hands on Annabelle's tummy. And Annabelle could experience that.

Alfie *wipes a few tears away from his eyes.*

Julie Remember when Annabelle kicked and you loved it? When you could sometimes see the ripple on my tummy when she moved. Annabelle was a proper night-time raver wasn't she? Just like her dad.

Alfie *nods, wipes his eyes and composes himself. He looks at* **Julie***.*

Alfie I'm sorry about my egregious, misplaced and erroneous cat analogy.

Julie What about your egregious, misplaced and erroneous cat analogy?

Alfie I feel like a bit of a berk.

Julie A bit of a berk?

Alfie A wally.

Julie A wally?

Alfie A monumental and major wally. I feel like it's the last night of Space. The closing fiesta. And it's me and Carl. And Carl can't find that Angie Stone record he loves. It's perfect. It's the perfect record to close out the season. But he can't find it.

Alfie *sings a bit of the melody.*

So he's like 'you play the last one, Alf'. And I'm like, hang on, Carl, hang on, mate. And he's like 'What?' And I'm like I've played all my records. There's nothing left in the box. And he's like 'you must have something, what's that?' And I'm like, that's a Max Bygraves . . .

Julie A what?

Alfie 'You're a pink toothbrush, I'm a blue toothbrush.'

Julie *laughs.*

Alfie But it's all I've got left in the box. It's my anxiety dream.

Julie That's your anxiety dream?

Alfie I clear the dancefloor and everyone hates me.

Julie No one hates you.

Alfie No?

Julie No one will hate you.

Alfie No?

Julie I love you. Of course I'll do what you want. If what you've said. It's how you want things to be at the end. Then I respect your wishes. Of course I do, babe.

Silence.

Alfie You know Space is closing permanently at the end of the season? End of an era that is.

Julie Space going at the end of the summer. Upton Park gone. It makes you wonder what else is around the corner, don't it, Alfie babe?

Alfie *thinks, tries to hold himself together.*

Alfie I don't want to die.

Julie I don't want you to die.

Alfie I love you.

Julie I love you more.

Alfie I love you more.

Julie Dickhead.

Alfie Twat.

Julie Fucking dickhead.

They look at each other for as long as you think you can get away with.

Alfie Maybe I can think about doing things a bit differently.

Julie It's your life.

Alfie It's not, it's our life.

Julie I think it is. It's your life and its precious. Don't you dare change your mind. Don't you dare.

Alfie When Annabelle comes we'll tell her I'm having some more Chemo.

Julie Will you?

Alfie Buy a bit more time. We'll tell her. We'll tell her whatever happens we'll all be together. Funny stories and pulling each other's legs.

Julie Do you really mean it, Alf?

Alfie Yeah, yeah, I do.

Julie What is it, love?

Alfie I hate cancer. I hate cancer more than I hate Millwall.

They look at each other.

Alfie *makes a decision. He goes to* **Julie** *and gets down on one knee.*

Julie Alf . . .

Alfie I'm sorry I'm a dickhead.

Julie Please babe, you've said sorry you don't have to do this any more . . . You're forgiven. I forgive you. I forgive you.

Alfie But will you marry me?

Julie What?

Alfie Will you marry me?

Julie *has a look around the room.*

Julie What?

Alfie It has been. It is. The greatest honour and privilege that you let me share my life with you. I love you with all my heart. And for always. I love you. If there's still time, will you marry me?

They look at each other for as long as you think you can get away with.

Julie No. We're alright as we are.

Alfie No?

Julie No.

Alfie What?

Julie Had you going there . . .

Alfie Where?

Julie Babe, joke. Joke, babe.

Alfie Oh.

Julie *laughs.* **Alfie** *laughs.*

Julie *gets down on her knees and hugs him and kisses him. They look at each other.*

Julie Of course I will. I love you.

Alfie Thank you, I love you.

They kiss. Julie's phone starts to ring in the kitchen. She gets up and goes and gets it.

Julie Hello babe, hello . . .

She comes back in.

It's Annabelle.

Alfie Ju . . .

Julie She's two minutes away.

Alfie For Christ's sake tell her to get off the phone . . .

Julie She's on the car speakerphone.

Julie *listens.* **Alfie** *feels uncomfortable but she's focused on Annabelle.*

Julie Alf, hang on, Toby's only got himself a shiner . . .

Alfie What?

Julie Went to see 'a show' in a funny little cabaret club with his mates. And the performer shot a mini vibrator out of her vagina. And bop. Copped it smack in the face.

She laughs.

Poor Toby . . .

Alfie Ju!

Julie Yes, I'll get the bacon on now. Yes, I know you like it crispy.

Julie *looks at* **Alfie** *and smiles.*

Julie Here, Annabelle, you'll never guess what? Your dad's just asked me to marry him.

She briefly holds the phone away from her ear.

I know. Better late than never. The old romantic's still down on one knee.

Alfie That's because I can't fucking get up.

Julie Oh . . . Listen babe, I'll see you in a minute.

She listens.

Listen, babe, we'll chat when you get here . . .

She listens, glances at **Alfie**.

Julie Thank you. Thank you. Yeah, we're over the moon.

She ends the call and puts the phone in her pocket. She goes to **Alfie** *and helps him up.*

Alfie Is she pleased?

Julie Very.

Alfie Are you?

Julie I am.

Alfie Will you help me talk to her? Will you help me explain I won't get better? All I've got is a bit more time.

They absorb this. Silence.

Julie She said 'are you getting married because there's really bad news?'

Alfie Did she?

Julie Are we?

Alfie At the end of the night. You play the best record in your box.

Julie I think so.

Alfie *looks around the room. Thinks about what lies ahead.*

Julie *nods and goes into the kitchen. She gets a frying pan out and on the hob.*

She takes the oil and gets some in the pan and takes the bacon from the fridge. She begins to heat the oil.

Alfie *takes his phone out and looks for something. He finds the song and presses play. 'Promised Land' by Joe Smooth plays.*

He can smell the bacon cooking. The doorbell goes. **Alfie** *turns off the music.* **Julie** *comes in from the kitchen.*

Silence.

Julie She'll be alright.

Alfie Will she?

Julie We'll tell her. We'll tell her we want a good end. And that's exactly what we're going to have.

The doorbell goes again. They look at each other for as long as you think you can get away with.

The doorbell goes again. **Julie**'s *phone starts to ring. They ignore it.*

Julie *goes to* **Alfie** *hugs him and kisses him and then heads out.* **Alfie** *composes himself, finds some courage and puts a smile on his face.*

End.

Discover. Read. Listen. Watch.

A NEW WAY TO ENGAGE WITH PLAYS

This award-winning digital library features over 3,000 playtexts, 400 audio plays, 300 hours of video and 360 scholarly books.

Playtexts published by Methuen Drama, The Arden Shakespeare, Faber & Faber, Playwrights Canada Press, Aurora Metro Books and Nick Hern Books.

Audio Plays from L.A. Theatre Works featuring classic and modern works from the oeuvres of leading American playwrights.

Video collections including films of live performances from the RSC, The Globe and The National Theatre, as well as acting masterclasses and BBC feature films and documentaries.

FIND OUT MORE:
www.dramaonlinelibrary.com • @dramaonlinelib

Methuen Drama Modern Plays

include

Bola Agbaje
Ayad Akhtar
Edward Albee
Jean Anouilh
John Arden
Peter Barnes
Clare Barron
Sebastian Barry
Alistair Beaton
Brendan Behan
Edward Bond
William Boyd
Bertolt Brecht
Howard Brenton
Amelia Bullmore
Anthony Burgess
Leo Butler
Jim Cartwright
Lolita Chakrabarti
Caryl Churchill
Lucinda Coxon
Tim Crouch
Shelagh Delaney
Ishy Din
Claire Dowie
David Edgar
David Eldridge
Dario Fo
Michael Frayn
John Godber
James Graham
David Greig
John Guare
Lauren Gunderson
Peter Handke
David Harrower
Jonathan Harvey
Robert Holman
David Ireland
Sarah Kane
Barrie Keeffe
Jasmine Lee-Jones
Anders Lustgarten
Duncan Macmillan
David Mamet
Patrick Marber
Martin McDonagh
Alistair McDowall
Arthur Miller
Tom Murphy
Phyllis Nagy
Anthony Neilson
Peter Nichols
Ben Okri
Joe Orton
Vinay Patel
Joe Penhall
Luigi Pirandello
Stephen Poliakoff
Lucy Prebble
Peter Quilter
Mark Ravenhill
Philip Ridley
Willy Russell
Sam Shepard
Martin Sherman
Chris Shinn
Jackie Sibblies Drury
Wole Soyinka
Simon Stephens
Kae Tempest
Laura Wade
Anne Washburn
Timberlake Wertenbaker
Roy Williams
Snoo Wilson
Theatre Workshop
Frances Ya-Chu Cowhig
Benjamin Zephaniah

Methuen Drama Student Editions

Alan Ayckbourn *Confusions* • **Mike Bartlett** *Earthquakes in London* • **Aphra Behn** *The Rover* • **Alice Birch** *Revolt. She Said. Revolt Again* • **Edward Bond** *Lear* • *Saved* • **Bertolt Brecht** *The Caucasian Chalk Circle* • *Fear and Misery in the Third Reich* • *The Good Person of Szechwan* • *Life of Galileo* • *Mother Courage and her Children* • *The Resistible Rise of Arturo Ui* • *The Threepenny Opera* • **Jon Brittain** *Rotterdam* • **Georg Büchner** *Woyzeck* • **Anton Chekhov** *The Cherry Orchard* • *The Seagull* • *Three Sisters* • *Uncle Vanya* • **Caryl Churchill** *Serious Money* • *Top Girls* • **Shelagh Delaney** *A Taste of Honey* • **Inua Ellams** *Barber Shop Chronicles* • **Euripides** *Elektra* • *Medea* • **Dario Fo** *Accidental Death of an Anarchist* • **Michael Frayn** *Copenhagen* • **John Galsworthy** *Strife* • **Nikolai Gogol** *The Government Inspector* • **Carlo Goldoni** *A Servant to Two Masters* • **James Graham** *This House* • **Tanika Gupta** *The Empress* • **Katori Hall** *The Mountaintop* • **Lorraine Hansberry** *A Raisin in the Sun* • **Robert Holman** *Across Oka* • **Henrik Ibsen** *A Doll's House* • *Ghosts* • *Hedda Gabler* • **Sarah Kane** *4.48 Psychosis* • *Blasted* • **Charlotte Keatley** *My Mother Said I Never Should* • **Dennis Kelly** *DNA* • **Bernard Kops** *Dreams of Anne Frank* • **Federico García Lorca** *Blood Wedding* • *Doña Rosita the Spinster* (bilingual edition) • *The House of Bernarda Alba* (bilingual edition) • *Yerma* (bilingual edition) • **David Mamet** *Glengarry Glen Ross* • *Oleanna* • **Patrick Marber** *Closer* • **John Marston** *The Malcontent* • **Martin McDonagh** *The Lieutenant of Inishmore* • *The Lonesome West* • *The Beauty Queen of Leenane* • *The Cripple of Inishmaan* • **Alistair McDowall** *Pomona* • **John McGrath** *The Cheviot, the Stag and the Black, Black Oil* • **Arthur Miller** *All My Sons* • *The Crucible* • *A View from the Bridge* • *Death of a Salesman* • *The Price* • *After the Fall* • *The Last Yankee* • *A Memory of Two Mondays* • *Broken Glass* • *Incident at Vichy* • *The American Clock* • *The Ride Down Mt. Morgan* • **Joe Orton** *Loot* • **Joe Penhall** *Blue/Orange* • **Luigi Pirandello** *Six Characters in Search of an Author* • **Lucy Prebble** *Enron* • **Mark Ravenhill** *Shopping and F***ing* • **Reginald Rose** *Twelve Angry Men* • **Willy Russell** *Blood Brothers* • *Educating Rita* • **Lemn Sissay** Benjamin Zephaniah's *Refugee Boy* • **Sophocles** *Antigone* • *Oedipus the King* • **Wole Soyinka** *Death and the King's Horseman* • **Simon Stephens** *Punk Rock* • *Pornography* • **Shelagh Stephenson** *The Memory of Water* • **August Strindberg** *Miss Julie* • **J. M. Synge** *The Playboy of the Western World* • **Kae Tempest** *Wasted* • **Theatre Workshop** *Oh What a Lovely War* • **Laura Wade** *Posh* • **Frank Wedekind** *Spring Awakening* • **Timberlake Wertenbaker** *Our Country's Good* • **Arnold Wesker** *The Merchant* • **Peter Whelan** *The Accrington Pals* • **Oscar Wilde** *The Importance of Being Earnest* • **Roy Williams** *Sing Yer Heart Out for the Lads* • **Tennessee Williams** *A Streetcar Named Desire* • *The Glass Menagerie* • *Cat on a Hot Tin Roof* • *Sweet Bird of Youth*

For a complete listing of
Methuen Drama titles, visit:
www.bloomsbury.com/drama

Follow us on Twitter and keep up to date
with our news and publications
@MethuenDrama